"Bragg offers an insightful look into the past and invites us all to look at the future of Indigenous affairs policy as well as the challenges and opportunities that lie ahead."

KEN WYATT AM MP

"At last, a pathway articulated by a Liberal to complete the unfinished business of liberalism in Australia."

RACHEL PERKINS

"Andrew Bragg is up for a fight: a fight for a more just Australia and he's taking on his own political tribe."

STAN GRANT

BURAADJA

THE LIBERAL CASE FOR
NATIONAL RECONCILIATION

ANDREW BRAGG

THE KAPUNDA PRESS

The Kapunda Press is an imprint of
CONNOR COURT PUBLISHING PTY LTD
PO Box 7257
Redland Bay QLD 4165

sales@connorcourt.com

www.connorcourt.com

Cover picture: Karen Gibson, *Rainy day fishing* (2021), acrylic on canvas.

ISBN: 9781922449542 (pbk.)

Cover design by Ian James.

Printed in Australia.

To John Brogden, Andrew Burnes, Sally Loane, Tony Shepherd, Warwick Smith, and Jennifer Westacott.

Mentoring is selfless and transformative.

Time is precious.

You paid it forward.

I will too.

bugiya *temp.*	Yesterday.
nhaway *temp.*	Today.
buraadja *temp.*	Tomorrow.

Patricia Ellis, Kerry Boyenga and Waine Donovan (eds)

Dhurga Dictionary and Learner's Grammar:
A south-east coast, NSW Aboriginal language

Contents

Foreword

The late Charles Perkins devoted his life to the advancement of Indigenous Australians. He often said, "We cannot live in the past, the past lives in us."

In all of us, the hopes, loves, losses, and traumas of our past live on in us. They linger, have a life of their own, and are passed on. It is true for individuals and it's true for countries.

Senator Andrew Bragg's book is a book of three parts: *bugiya, nhaway,* and *buraadja*—yesterday, today, and tomorrow. It seeks to answer the question: how do we take our past and present, and use it to build a better tomorrow?

I believe a better tomorrow must mean engaging with what I call a national truth and a national shame: that our Aboriginal and Torres Strait Islander children in Australia today do not have the same opportunities as all other children growing up in Australia. They never have in Australia. Despite good intentions, it is our truth and shame. That is at the core of this book.

In a way that is reminiscent of Billy Wentworth, Ian Viner, and Fred Chaney, Andrew Bragg has spent considerable time listening to Indigenous people. To his considerable credit, he has seriously engaged with the belief I expressed in the 2020 Closing the Gap speech. Namely, that for over two centuries we have perpetuated and suffered from an ingrained way of thinking, and that is the belief we know better than our Indigenous peoples. We don't.

We also thought we understood the problems facing Indigenous

Australians better than they did. We don't.

If we are truly to change, then we must address the areas of disadvantage, not from our point of view, but from the viewpoint of Indigenous Australians before we can hope to make a real difference. Unless we do so—our good intentions, our good faith, will continue to amount to little.

That approach of 'listening with' not 'doing to' is the approach the Government is taking as we work with Indigenous leaders (known as the Coalition of Peaks). It is the path I am committed to.

This book is Andrew Bragg's journey so far—an empathetic and thoughtful reflection of how we can heal our country's greatest fracture—and then deliver a *buraadja* worthy of us all. Andrew rightly has not prescribed 'the way forward' but he has engaged thoughtfully with our *bugiya, nhaway*, and *buraadja*. Not all of us will agree with every reflection or conclusion, but the book allows us to think and engage on the questions of who we are as Australians and who we want to be.

2021 marks the fiftieth anniversary of Liberal Senator Neville Bonner taking his place as the first Indigenous Australian in the Australian Parliament. It is an anniversary that all Liberals, and indeed, all Australians should honour and celebrate. *Buraadja* is a worthy contribution to the commemorations we will have during 2021.

Scott Morrison

Prime Minister

April 2021

Acknowledgements

I have many people to thank and I must start with my editor—the brilliant, generous, and thoughtful Damien Freeman. He is, like Bill Wentworth in some ways, very much a radical liberal on Indigenous issues who pushes liberals to think again and to do more. He has now spent a large part of his life making a serious and practical contribution to the debate on constitutional reform. His contribution assured; he has helped others like me who want to help the debate move to a point where a change is more likely to happen. He has been generous with his time, counsel, and resources. This book would not be possible without him. The other person I must thank at the outset is Professor Tom Frame who helped me come up with the concept of a book on liberalism and Indigenous policy. The organization Freeman established with my colleague, Julian Leeser MP, known as Uphold & Recognise has done so much good work. I am very grateful to the chairman of Uphold & Recognise, Sean Gordon, who has taken me to a number of Indigenous communities in New South Wales, including his hometown of Brewarrina. Sean is warm, smart, and respected in both Canberra and Brewarrina. No mean feat.

John Mangos in my office has helped enormously with this book. He has pulled together research, undertaken invaluable community engagement, and helped me with the endless details of the manuscript. Like Damien, John is passionate about Indigenous Australia. He has lifelong Indigenous friends and is widely respected. This task has weighed heavily on my office without undermining the work we do for the people of New South Wales, and I must acknowledge the contribution of Nick Healy, Hunter Wardman, and Deyi Wu.

A number of great Australians read the manuscript and helped me fashion it into something cogent. I am indebted to Chris Puplick AM in particular for reading multiple drafts. Thank you to David Bold, Hamish Bragg, Sam Fay, Danny Gilbert AM, Sean Gordon, Stan Grant, Julian Leeser MP, Rachel Perkins, Josh Riley, Kathryn Smith, Warwick Smith AO, Peta Seaton, and the Hon. Ken Wyatt AM MP for reading the manuscript and offering feedback. It was Danny Gilbert who first drove my engagement on this issue. He has made such an important contribution. He is a great leader. A special thanks goes to my friends, Warwick Smith AO, Sam Hallinan, and Greg O'Neill OAM for their support for this project. I also acknowledge the PM Glynn Institute at Australian Catholic University for making me a visiting fellow in order to support this project.

There are also dozens who gave their time to be interviewed or to provide some comment for the record. I have interviewed a wide range of Indigenous people as well as policymakers going back to the Menzies era. Being able to secure historically valuable material from the likes of John Moriarty AM, Tony Eggleton, and Ian Sinclair has been a humbling exercise. I only hope that this book encourages others to dig into the rich history of Australian liberalism.

I must also thank my parliamentary colleagues, especially the leadership, for encouraging me to produce a book like this. It is clear that many of my colleagues would not agree with elements of this book. But the existence of this book shows that liberalism is alive and well inside the Liberal Party.

There is no doubt we Liberals are bad at documenting our own contribution. My hope is the words in this book, and also the images, convey the full picture. Accordingly, I am indebted to the institutions and the individuals which provided permission to reproduce these valuable snapshots of Australian history.

Further embedding Indigenous culture into our national life is highly desirable. That's why I wanted to use the Dhurga language for the title of this book which has been brought back to life by the Yuin people of the south coast of New South Wales. This is a great story of the rebirth of language. Craig Ritchie at the Australian Institute of Aboriginal and Torres Strait Islander Studies (AIATSIS) helped facilitate this outcome and I thank him deeply. Craig traveled with me to Moruya to meet with Yuin Traditional Owner Patricia Ellis who co-authored the Dhurga dictionary. Patricia kindly provided her blessing for the use of the Dhurga language. Meeting with Patricia was a highlight of this process.

The magnificent artwork on the front of this book was created by Kuku Yalanji and Kuku Nyungkul woman Karen Gibson. It is called *Rainy day fishing*, which, in Karen's words, is basically the time when, after the rain has flooded the rivers with fresh water, the ladies would go and throw a line near the bank in order to catch the fish because, at this time, the current is so strong and the fish swim close to the bank. The line is set resting on the waters which you see in the artwork. The dots represent the raindrops, the blue in the background is fresh river waters. Karen started painting on canvas in 1984 and considers herself a self-taught artist. Her work is magnificent, and I am honoured to have *Rainy day fishing* on the cover. I am grateful to Cape York Wuthathi Yupungathi man Richie Ahmat who connected me to Karen. Richie came to Canberra for my First Speech to the Senate along with Rachel Perkins. I am fortunate to count both as friends.

Finally, I owe my family an apology. After promising I wouldn't write another book this term, I decided this was too important and couldn't wait. I thank Melanie, Sophia, and James for their patience. Too often the benches and desks have been covered with papers and I have been tapping away on my computer, thereby breaking the serenity. As I have reflected in this book, I have so much hope for my children to live in a reconciled Australia. We have made progress upon reconciliation in my lifetime but there is much more to do.

Andrew Bragg, Sydney, 2 April 2021

Prologue

URAADJA MEANS TOMORROW in the Dhurga (*Doo-roo-ga*) language used by the Yuin people from the south coast of New South Wales. The traditional owners have developed a dictionary of Dhurga language which provides an opportunity to use these words which may otherwise have been lost. I thank them. *Buraadja* is about a better tomorrow just as Yolngu leader Galarrway Yunupingu (from North Eastern Arnhem Land in the Northern Territory) wished for "a happy ending to this story" in his searing essay, *Tradition, truth and tomorrow*. Australia is a great country, but it has not been a great country for Aboriginal people or Torres Strait Islanders. This book sets out an agenda for national reconciliation.

Australians need to care more; we need to listen more, and we need to deliver. The nation has not delivered for Indigenous people and we have been too comfortable about it. Australia has been too comfortable with the gap in life expectancy and social and economic outcomes between Indigenous and other Australians. *Buraadja* offers a plan to deliver national reconciliation by enacting the Uluru Statement from the Heart along with practical and symbolic changes designed to close the economic and social gaps between Indigenous people and the rest of the Australian population, and further to embed Aboriginal and Torres Strait Islander cultures in our national life. The Uluru Statement of 2017 is the great opportunity Australia has to complete the national project. The Statement sits at the heart of national reconciliation and at the heart of this book. The Indigenous Voice is Uluru's centrepiece. A Voice would be a transformative reform for our country structurally, practically, and symbolically.

Our education system has made much progress in presenting the full picture of our history, but our national life does not reflect the richness of this country's complete history. If we make these changes, we would "complete our Commonwealth" without taking anything from any other Australian, in the words of Noel Pearson, a lawyer, academic, and land rights activist from the Guggu Yalanji people of the rainforest regions of far north Queensland. This nation is home to the oldest continuing culture on earth.

I write this book as a sitting member of the Australian Parliament, as a Senator who is a member of the Liberal Party, which makes me a partisan. My objective is to set out a case so that liberal and conservative voters can support reconciliation and the Uluru Statement. In setting out the liberal case for national reconciliation, I have avoided politicking because we need to work together. Both major parties have delivered signature achievements in Indigenous affairs. Nevertheless, collectively we have not been successful at delivering for Indigenous people.

In writing this book, I don't seek to speak for anyone other than myself. Certainly, I do not seek to speak for Indigenous people. I represent almost 300,000 Indigenous people in the Senate, so it is important that I have a working knowledge of the major issues affecting them. As I have learned writing this book, I am still learning to be an advocate for Indigenous people. My lessons will never end, but I am determined to continue learning all that I can about Australia's Indigenous cultures. Equally, I do not claim to speak for the federal government or the Liberal Party of which I am a member.

The views expressed here are my views forged from many interviews, research, and reading. I have conducted more than two dozen interviews, half with Indigenous people. I know some people will be uncomfortable or unhappy about the way I have set out this history and the agenda. But, in order to gain momentum, I firmly believe that we have to move beyond the talking points. That is what this book seeks to do.

Introduction
Four whys

THIS IS A BOOK of three parts—history, listening, and the future. That is, yesterday, today, and tomorrow. In the Dhurga language, this means *bugiya*, *nhaway*, and *buraadja*. The first chapter chiefly sets out the policy contribution of the liberal and conservative side of politics—as well as the failures. This is designed to remind the Australian liberal movement of the sizable legacy of former prime ministers Harold Holt and Malcolm Fraser and their governments. The second chapter considers the current state of Indigenous policy and evaluates the reform proposals seeking to address these issues. The third chapter culminates in a policy offering on national reconciliation.

National reconciliation is, put simply, the nation coming to an accomodation with Indigenous people through national institutions, including the Constitution and the Parliament of the Commonwealth. It is about making good with Indigenous people and delivering a substantial reconciliation which contains both practical and symbolic components. Reconciliation should be anchored in the 2017 Uluru Statement from the Heart, which sets out a multifaceted policy to achieve a reconciliation. Yet reconciliation isn't about one particular policy. It is a broad suite which includes delivering on the Closing the Gap framework as well as economic development, and the need to address symbolic issues in a cohesive approach. All the discussions I have had with Indigenous people in New South Wales reinforce the reality that national reconciliation is necessary in order to close the gap. This is the position in Nowra, Redfern, Bourke, and Kempsey. We need to tackle the social problems, but it is virtually impossible for a Commonwealth Government to do this until the people concerned feel reconciled to the Commonwealth, accept its legitimacy, and want to work with it to solve their problems. Therefore, the national reconciliation set out in *Buraadja* is about delivering a comprehensive package of changes. There is a difference between practical and symbolic reconciliation. Practical reconciliation might be found in legislating a local community engagement structure or 'Voice', whereas symbolic reconciliation might be a statement of acknowledgement about Indigenous Australia in the nation's Constitution. Too often, debates on Indigenous policy are presented as a choice between national issues, such as the status of Australia Day, and community issues, such as high levels of incarceration. This is a false choice which conceals the genuine complexity.

In part, it depends on your perspective. For the booming middle classes of Indigenous Australia, it is possible that the symbolic needs are greater than for community members who are struggling without an education or gainful employment. All of it is important for us to move forward together. The nation is capable of setting out a fulsome agenda on national reconciliation. We can walk and chew gum. We can, for example, address false narratives in the national anthem just as we pursue the agreed Closing the Gap measures on childhood education. But it must be well documented that there is a plan; that there is an agenda which is complete and in parts interdependent. That is what this book seeks to do in a comprehensive fashion.

In doing so, I address four questions at the outset: Why this issue? Why now? Why me? And, why the Liberal Party?

Why this issue and why does Indigenous affairs matter?

How do I, as a liberal, justify the proposition that Indigenous people should garner special attention?

Some liberals think liberalism and Indigenous affairs are in permanent conflict. This juxtaposition has been disingenuously amplified by the opponents of the 2017 Uluru Statement who argue an Indigenous Voice to Parliament would be fundamentally illiberal. On face value, an institution closed to 97% of Australians sounds illiberal. But this ignores the history of Australia and the present where the only broadscale race-based laws exist for Indigenous Australians.[1] Liberalism only works if everyone is given an equal chance, and, for 250 years, we have not worked hard enough to guarantee the liberal deal for all Australians.

Australian liberalism is a philosophy for a system of government and for making laws and policies. It promotes freedom, individual agency, tolerance, and the private economy. It is classless and designed to allow people to rise as far as their talents will take them. It is a product of the seventeenth and eighteenth-century Enlightenment. The theory of liberalism was influential in the creation of the Australian project, which was a desire to establish a society which was more liberal than the European societies from which the settlers had travelled. This meant economic and social freedom for settlers to pursue their own goals outside of the class-based society that was commonplace in Europe.

In the 1940s, Sir Robert Menzies set out a formula in his "forgotten people" speeches, which laid the foundations of the modern Liberal Party of which I am a representative. Menzies said, "we took the name Liberal because we were determined to be a progressive party, willing to make experiments in no sense reactionary but believing in the individual, his rights and his enterprise . . ."[2] The best account of Australian liberalism is the history written by former Liberal minister David Kemp.[3] Kemp writes, "Liberals saw the road to a classless society through the promotion of an egalitarian democratic culture, broadening the ownership of private property, universal education and politics that secured the equal freedom of all to pursue their own goals in life."[4] Australian liberalism should work for all Australians—yet it was not designed for Indigenous people. That has been well documented as the nation has sought to redress past wrongs in recent decades. The problem for the Indigenous people was partly that they were, at best, on the fringes of society, and, moreover, that they were the target of racism. Liberalism and racism coexisted. As a consequence, a bedrock of liberalism—private property—was seized from Indigenous people without payment.

The foundational offence of liberal Australia was to pursue the development of modern Australia on the back of the displacement of Indigenous people. The history of the nation was cast without these people. They were regarded as little more than a footnote about the pre-history of Australia. A 'dying race' expected to expire in time. The national blindness gave rise to the Great Australian Silence that the anthropologist and historian, Bill Stanner, spoke of in his 1968 Boyer lectures, *After the Dreaming*. Stanner's critique of Australian history was that it had pretended that Indigenous people did not exist. Stanner's formulation was that it was easier to be silent about this great national shame and quiet about the stain on the nation's canvas which was otherwise very successful. In the decades following Stanner's lectures, the history of Australia has been rebalanced but, as a liberal Enlightenment project, Australia is yet to deliver for Indigenous people. The truth is liberalism can work for Indigenous people.

Today's statistics on Indigenous life expectancy, education levels, incarceration, and health outcomes speak to the challenge. The Indigenous disadvantage is entrenched in modern Australia. I, therefore, pose the counter question. As a liberal, how can I not spend the precious time I have in public office trying to ensure a liberal Australia works for all Australians? I think we should advance structural reforms which the Indigenous community has sought—because it will make Australia better. It would make Australia better on the inside and out. Stan Grant, an Indigenous historian, broadcaster, and Wiradjuri man from central New South Wales, told me, "There'll be a lack of national legitimacy until we fix it." We all know it to be true. It must be why John Howard said in 2007, when he was prime minister. "I believe we must find room in our national life to formally recognise the special status of Aboriginal [peoples] and Torres Strait Islanders as the first peoples of our nation."

My sense is that this is such a troubled debate because most Australians have a limited understanding of the issues facing Indigenous people, along with limited engagement, or none at all. Indigenous people and 'their issues' do not feature in the lives of most Australians. This is the wicked problem of proximity. As Stan Grant says, "People don't know us." This is a product of scale and dispersion. It is a small group in a big country. Of the 25 million Australians, fewer than 3% of Australians are Indigenous. Almost one quarter live in very remote areas and the majority live in suburbs, towns, and cities. In a Commonwealth like ours, their issues are our issues.

The failure to make good is the biggest drag on our nation's identity. I think that Noel Pearson, an Indigenous activist from Cape York, is probably the best thinker about our national identity. I reflected on his counsel to me before my First Speech to the Senate in 2019, when he said "Andrew, this is my country too." Pearson's 2014 essay, *A Rightful Place*,[5] has influenced me more than any other text on the issue. In it, he says that "you cannot have a unified nation, this cannot be a fair nation, without the proper inclusion of three per cent of the nation who were originally excluded from the Constitution." Pearson's pitch is underpinned by a desire to complete the Australian project—which remains the most potent pitch to all Australians—especially to liberals and conservatives.

Why now?

The Black Lives Matter protests of 2020 should jolt us into further consideration of our history, our own cohesion, and our policy response. Indigenous incarceration has been on the national policy agenda for at least the last thirty years, after the 1987-1991 Royal Commission into Aboriginal Deaths in Custody. This debate significantly predates Black Lives Matter, which is a movement of mainly African Americans aggrieved by their treatment at the hands of the American state and its constituent parts. It was supercharged following the death of an African American man George Floyd at the hands of a police officer with his knee on Floyd's neck in May 2020. Following Floyd's death, protests occurred in Australian cities under the Black Lives Matter banner in solidarity with African Americans, but also to express concern about high levels of Indigenous incarceration in Australia.

I developed a view that the issues underlying Black Lives Matter were both legitimate and needed to be addressed in Australia. Some Australians only saw the negative side of the protests. I saw the opportunity to strive again for national reconciliation. This does not mean that I agree with the tactics used by the protestors. Black Lives Matter originates from a different perspective and a different country with a different historical backdrop. Supplanting a movement from a different country does not mean the issues the United States faces are the same issues as those we face in Australia. However, the reality is that, in a crude comparison between African Americans and Indigenous Australians, we have not performed well.

Black Lives Matter may be imported but it has a local resonance that few Australians noticed. Perhaps that is because Australians take history for granted. Australia's modern history is nothing short of epic. In a relatively short period of time, Australia developed into a nation with a vibrant liberal democracy underpinned by the rule of law and an economic system which has catapulted a nation with a small population to be the twelfth largest economy. The nation has the strongest possible foundation upon which to address our issues. As the Covid-19 pandemic has proven, Australia's institutions are amongst the world's very best.

There has been a price for Australia taking its history for granted. That price has been paid by the Indigenous people. Stan Grant's diagnosis is that "Australians are not historically introspective because we think it is self-indulgent. We are an Enlightenment nation. Cook and Philip were Enlightenment people. You left your history behind. This is a virtue, it has been fundamental to our success. But it doesn't work for us. My blood is in the soil. Not at Gallipoli." It is true that Grant's family's blood is not at Gallipoli, but more than fifty Aboriginal soldiers did serve at Gallipoli, where thirteen died.

The data proves the underlying issues are genuine. On incarceration rates, the Bureau of Justice Statistics of the United States Department of Justice quotes 2,207 African Americans are incarcerated per 100,000 head of population, compared with the Australian Bureau of Statistics figure of 2,346 Indigenous Australians per 100,000 head of population.[6] Equally, the average life expectancy of an African American is higher than an Indigenous Australian. I appeared on ABC's Q&A program in the weeks immediately following the death of George Floyd and the emergence of Black Lives Matter. As I said in that broadcast, Australia is a great country, but it has not been a great country for Indigenous people. It was not a rehearsed line but the more I think about it, the more I think it is a fair summary of things. Australia has been a great refuge for people from all over the world. We have built a nation with very strong institutions which have enabled us to maintain amongst the world's best living standards. But our success has occurred in part at the expense and by the exclusion of Indigenous people, and I am worried that Australia's failure to deliver for Indigenous Australians will continue to undermine the nation.

Money has been expended but the statistics remain bad and the unrest continues—at last count, $33 billion was spent on Indigenous policy programs per annum. Yet the outcomes remain poor. The Uluru Statement was delivered in 2017. It is a great opportunity for Australian patriots. It sets out concepts which would help consolidate Australia. It would allow us to deliver something important for Indigenous people and for our country. I don't want to see it sink into the sand like the Barunga Statement, which sought more control and agency for Indigenous people when it was presented to the prime minister, Bob Hawke, in 1988. I have followed the various debates closely over the years and, once elected to the Senate in 2019, I decided I would spend time and political capital to advance the agenda. I thought carefully about what I would address in my First Speech to the Senate in July 2019.

A First Speech is the one opportunity you are afforded as a member of federal parliament to set out a long-term view of your priorities. I identified economic policy and Indigenous matters as my two priorities. I told the Senate:

> I am also a supporter of constitutional recognition. The latest chapter in this long journey is the Uluru Statement. It offers a challenge to our country. The Uluru Statement says: "we seek Constitutional reforms to empower our people and take a rightful place in our own country." It imagines a Constitution where Indigenous Australians are guaranteed a say on laws made under the races and territories powers which affect them. Uluru asks legislators to consult Indigenous people on the laws which are relevant to them. This is a good idea. This is a fair idea. But I would not support constitutional recognition at any price.

In this First Speech, I set out five requirements for successfully implementing the Uluru Statement:

- Capturing the broad support of the Indigenous community;

- Focusing on community level improvements;
- Maintaining the supremacy of parliament;
- Maintaining the value of equality; and
- Strengthening national unity.

Focusing on the group which are the most imprisoned, the most likely to die young or suffer debilitating health problems is necessary. It is urgent work. I acknowledge that some Liberal Party colleagues are uncomfortable with the agenda, but we have legislated separate arrangements for Indigenous people since 1788. We have talked about the symbolic and the practical issues facing the nation for too long. We have already spent nearly fifteen years talking about constitutional recognition after John Howard put it on the agenda in 2007. The clock is ticking.

Why me?

I am not Indigenous but I am Australian. Australia is my country. I am a liberal and a patriot. If liberalism is about giving everyone their best shot, patriotism is about being proud of one's country. It's about loving your country. I love my country. It has given my family a far better life than would have been possible in the 'old country'. My father, a migrant from the United Kingdom, was the first person in our family who received a tertiary education. The rise of our family has been thanks to Australia—we owe a debt to the nation. It's a debt I hope to repay through advocacy and delivery on this policy agenda.

I care for Australia and I worry that we have not delivered on national reconciliation. I have known and know many Indigenous Australians. I went to school with Indigenous kids and I played country football with them. I grew up in the town of Shepparton in northern Victoria on Yorta Yorta country. Its Indigenous powerhouse was the Rumbalara Club. I remember being resentful about a grant given to an Indigenous group which allowed it to purchase a hovercraft. I was unhappy that my family was not issued with a hovercraft. I was resentful for what I saw as a special deal. I am certain that I engaged in casual racism. I have often reflected upon that hovercraft and my response to its existence. I am certain my shallow understanding and engagement led me to an erroneous position.

Attending public and local Catholic schools in Shepparton in the 1990s, there was very basic acknowledgement of the nation's long history. I took an elective in year 11 to study history. I remember it was a tiny class. The year 11 award for history was the only academic award I ever received. In this tiny class, we were provided with a balanced view of Victorian (but not Australian) history. It presented the issues from both the settler and Indigenous perspectives. My honest assessment is that this study did not significantly alter my view about what I saw as a special deal for Aboriginals. I am certain that external events did not change my position as a high school student. In 2000, when I was in year 10, there was a march across the Sydney Harbour Bridge to promote reconciliation. Similar marches occurred in Melbourne and other cities. This did not register in my mind in Shepparton.

I later moved to Canberra to study at the Australian National University. Attending university in Canberra opened my eyes to a much bigger world than I had experienced in small town Victoria. ANU was a melting pot. I have often joked that moving from Shepparton to Canberra felt like moving to Hollywood. I made lifelong friends at university, but it also changed my perspective on Indigenous Australia. One afternoon, I was driving with friends past the Aboriginal Tent Embassy and I suggested that it was not a good institution and we should make our feelings known. One of my conservative friends said firmly in response that he *supported their cause*. That was the turning point for me to reassess my attitude. I can't say exactly what it was about those words, but I realised I needed to think carefully about the issues. And I did. While I don't particularly enjoy reciting that particular incident, it is, I suspect, a common perspective from middle Australia.

As the years stretched on, I took the time to listen to the issues raised by Indigenous Australians. I got to know Indigenous Australians in adulthood much better than I did as a child. The message I heard was clear: "paternalism is bad, and our communities need capacity-building." There is still too much being "done to us—not by us or with us." When I arrived at the Business Council of Australia as an executive director in charge of membership, I was surprised that the person running Indigenous engagement was not an Indigenous person. I was determined to appoint an Indigenous person when given the chance. I appointed Josh Riley, a Wiradjuri man from central New South Wales, who was working in Canada in economic development policy. He has become a friend and I am very pleased the Morrison government has decided to appoint Josh to an overseas posting. He will be a great representative of Australia and our interests.

I want to do the same again and use the platform I have been given by the people of New South Wales and the Liberal Party to advance this agenda. I have this platform now and I want to use it to work on reconciliation for a more cohesive country. In effect, the job is to listen to and advocate on behalf of the most dispersed minority in Australia. One of the most meaningful roles I have taken on in my career thus far was to lead the 2017 campaign by Liberals & Nationals for Yes on same-sex marriage. This public campaign occurred after the Turnbull government decided to conduct a postal survey of Australians on the question of whether the marriage laws should be changed to accommodate same-sex marriage. This unconventional approach was required as the Senate had blocked the commitment the Turnbull government took to the 2016 election to hold a plebiscite on same-sex marriage.

A group of government backbenchers who wanted to bring marriage equality to a head asked me to take on the role. They included Trevor Evans MP, Senator Dean Smith, Tim Wilson MP, and Trent Zimmerman MP. The national campaign was needed to win the postal survey so that same-sex marriage could be legalised in Australia. I would run a distinctly branded and organized campaign alongside the primary Equality campaign. When I was asked to take on the role in August 2017, before the High Court cleared the survey for takeoff the following month, I was in two minds. I had been through a bruising phase of my career as acting federal director of the Liberal Party and the idea of taking on an uncertain campaign that might fail was scary. On the other hand, I passionately felt that the law excluding my fellow Australians from civil marriage was illiberal. That had been my position for as long as I could remember. In the end, I decided to take on the challenge, knowing that this was important to so many Australians and it would say a lot about the type of country we live in. The result was a majority of people in 71 of 76 Coalition seats voting yes. A remarkable outcome. The Libs & Nats for Yes campaign was not about rainbow flags. It was about families and fairness. This taught me a good deal about campaigning for social change in middle Australia.

The issues relating to Indigenous constitutional matters are very different, but the sense of advocating for a positive change that will benefit a minority that will not harm the majority is the same. There is one very important parallel. Looking back on the campaign against marriage equality, led by the Coalition for Marriage, there were promises (perhaps threats) that the sky would fall in if marriage equality became a reality. As academic and author Louise Richardson-Self said, "For example, the Coalition for Marriage, perhaps the most visible body behind the 'No' campaign, adopted three argumentative strategies: the first, an argument regarding changes to sex education and parents' rights; the second, a free speech argument; and the third, an argument concerning freedom of religion."[7]

Three years on, the lived experience is that parents' rights are not linked to the Marriage Act; freedom of speech is still a right, unless inciting hate, and churches can marry who they want. Inevitably, there will be a rerun of this approach with different arguments when it comes to a future referendum question. I want to use this experience to support a change which will significantly improve the experience of a minority without taking anything from the majority. In fact, the delivery of Noel Pearson's "more complete Commonwealth" has significant benefits for the majority— cohesion, stability, and common purpose.

Under our constitutional arrangements, every voter has a say in a referendum, so a large component of the 97% of non-Indigenous Australians must be engaged for any change to become reality.

The Constitution demands a majority of people and a majority of States must approve an amendment to the Constitution. This double majority has been achieved only eight times in the past 120 years; the last time was in 1977. This numeric reality is one hard-headed reason to explain why I would take such an interest in these matters. Many more supporters who are not Indigenous will be needed. As Noel Pearson says, "This must by definition be a unifying cause. If we don't have an argument that can persuade 90% of the nation, then the cause of constitutional reform is lost."

The 3% of the nation will always be a minority. Being a voice for minorities is an important part of the liberal tradition and something that I believe in strongly. I do not believe that there are many votes at stake—perhaps there are only votes to lose as the reconciliation leader and Labor Senator Patrick Dodson, a Yawuru man from the Kimberley Region of Western Australia, said, "The priority on the (Australian) government's side of the equation has been about securing the non-Aboriginal voters."[8] Yet the way I think about it is that a majority of Australians could give something to Indigenous Australians which will cost them nothing but do so much good for the nation.

Why the liberal approach?

The unifying approach which Pearson sets out is the only credible pathway. Although to some extent this agenda is about correcting past misdeeds, it is also about the future and our national unity. Tearing down modern Australia will not work. It won't deliver votes at a referendum. A significant component of the reforms sought by Indigenous Australians and by me would require constitutional amendments. This means asking a majority of the nation to vote in favour of changes for a group of Australians not personally known to them.

In crude terms, the only way to deliver the reforms sought through the Uluru Statement is for the changes to be unifying and patriotic in nature. They cannot be seen as divisive; as conferring exclusive rights or undermining the Australian project. This agenda should appeal to conservatives in particular as a natural liberal-conservative position is to value heritage and tradition—including Indigenous heritage. There are four main reasons I think only the Liberal-National Coalition in government can deliver this change.

First, the liberal approach to policymaking. Australian liberalism provides an awning under which all Australians can find a cool place in the shade. I regret that the awning of Australian liberalism and Indigenous policy seems smaller because few people know of the contributions of Australian liberalism like voting rights, land rights, and referendum success. Australian liberalism is flexible enough to deal with Indigenous affairs in the twenty-first century. The historical and legal reality means that there are issues that need to be addressed in order for Indigenous people to be able to enjoy the freedom that other Australians do. It remains the case that Indigenous people are the only Australians who have a slew of laws made specifically for them. Flexibility is at the core of Australian liberalism, as Menzies said in describing the Liberal Party's approach "we have no doctrinaire political philosophy".[9] The history of the Liberal Party in government has shown that policies to address Indigenous affairs have been regularly deployed which, although heavily resisted at the time, have withstood the test of time.

A liberal approach to national reconciliation is to maintain fidelity to the key tenets of Australian liberalism—rule of law, freedom, and individual dynamism whilst recognising that the need for special laws demands special systems. At the moment, we have special laws for Indigenous people but no system to reflect this reality. The flexible beauty of liberalism is that it can adapt, even if it is tardy. The most relevant philosophy to draw upon is the slogan from the American Revolution, "no taxation without representation." How could you have special laws drawn up without some special capacity to engage the affected people? That's the system we have today in Australia.

Policies like land rights have become part of the Australian project and have been further embedded into the common law and statute books. The question for today is whether these policies are promoting the economic development and individual agency that we hold dear under the liberal formula. The point about land rights and native title, the former having been legislated by a Liberal Government, is crucial to any discussion about Indigenous affairs and liberalism. On face value, the basic philosophy of liberalism to drive individualism is inconsistent with Indigenous collectivism. Our system of government has been flexible enough to accommodate collectivism and we have established institutions in our liberal democracy to manage this inconsistency. There are land councils established under Commonwealth and State law, as well as the National Native Title Tribunal which deals with native title applications. This means that Indigenous groups and nations have had legal status at Commonwealth law from the 1976 passage of the Land Rights Act by the Fraser government. This is not an endorsement of the detailed operation of the land rights system which, as this book sets out, appears to have shortcomings. Beyond the statute book, the common law has developed a legal definition of an Indigenous Australian in the 1992 *Mabo* case, which is relevant to any legal consideration of Indigenous policy matters.

The system of Australian liberalism which has proven to be flexible enough to recognise collective Indigenous groups cannot stretch so far as creating a degree of privilege for Indigenous peoples. There are limits to liberalism and this would be illiberal. A preview of this can be seen in the High Court's judgement in *Love v Commonwealth* (2020), in which people not born in Australia, but who claimed Aboriginal heritage, sought to avoid deportation orders after committing crimes in Australia. *Mabo* was invoked. The tripartite definition of Aboriginality from *Mabo* was used as the basis to set aside the orders. This definition is: "a person self-identifying as an Aboriginal person, showing descent from Aboriginal ancestors and demonstrating that people enjoying traditional authority in that person's Aboriginal community recognise the person as a member of the community."[10]

This *Mabo* definition was used by four of the seven High Court justices to argue that Aboriginal Australians had unique rights under our legal system and it wasn't for parliament to use its powers to exclude people as "aliens" under the Constitution if they have Indigenous heritage. The Chief Justice, Susan Kiefel, dissented and said:

> So understood, (under this new formula) the rule is of the nature of a right which would inhere in the person regardless of the person's status as a non-citizen and as a citizen of a foreign sovereign state and regardless of their lack of relationship with the body politic of the Commonwealth of Australia . . . (and) race is irrelevant to the questions of citizenship and membership of the Australian body politic.

In other words, conferring a special right of residence on Indigenous persons, which is unavailable to others, is ridiculous. It is unfair and not how citizenship laws can work in a world where there has been mass migration for centuries. For the purposes of this debate, the *Love* case only provokes concern that constitutional changes could give rise to judicial activism which would undermine our liberal democracy. If the judiciary can confer, erroneously, in the words of the Chief Justice, a new category of citizenship by applying principles from native title into a case on citizenship, wouldn't the risk only increase if the Constitution was amended? Anything that seems illiberal, like this judgement, would not be supported by Australians at a referendum.

The history of Australian liberalism and Indigenous affairs demonstrates the flexibility of liberalism. But it is only by understanding the history that liberal policymakers can develop an historically informed approach to Indigenous policy. Only an historically informed approach presents any hope of successful policy in this area. Indigenous affairs presents a unique challenge to the liberal policymaker as it must be historically informed in a way that other aspects of policymaking may not always require.

Secondly, federalism and representation. It is important to take the citizens of the smaller States into account. A referendum on components of Uluru risks winning a majority of the popular vote, largely in Sydney and Melbourne, but failing to win four of the six required States. The beauty of the Coalition is that it is represented by vastly different people from all walks of life across our nation.

To say there are different views on this issue inside my party would be an understatement. There is significant external focus on the diverse views within the Liberal Party—that is legitimate and healthy. A party which blends a strong tradition of both executive and backbench policy leadership is a live, functioning body of people. I observed in my first eighteen months in public office a huge gulf in culture on backbench engagement in policy between the two major parties. I am confident that a properly ventilated proposal could win the support of the vast majority of Coalition members.

Thirdly, patriotism. Our party is a party which embraces patriotism, as a love of country—with all its significant achievements and correctable faults taken together. The Liberal Party is the party of tradition, and liberalism and patriotism are part of that tradition, even though they might sometimes be at odds. Unless this agenda is seen as an agenda to build on and consolidate the Australian ideal, it is dead. If there is any sense that this is a vote of no confidence in Australia, any referendum has no chance. The Greens, in contrast to the Liberal Party, are much more likely to entertain unpatriotic stunts like moving Australia Day—which would be a denial of our history.

Australia has a history which has been both good and bad. 26 January 1788 happened. It cannot unhappen. The day should be a true reflection of Australian culture using Noel Pearson's formula: an Indigenous heritage, British institutions, and a multicultural tenor which has enriched us all. Australians love Australia, this is particularly true amongst migrants. Patriotic language, with which the left is generally uncomfortable, would be essential for national reconciliation to succeed. The reform agenda needs to be a consolidation of the Australian project, not the destruction of it. Australia is up for the honest conversation which starts with the simple reflection Stan Grant made to me, namely that "history is worn lightly in Australia but that doesn't work for Indigenous people."

Fourthly, history. If we can reclaim the lost history of Holt, we can write another chapter in our long journey of advancing Australia. Harold Holt was a great prime minister who delivered an historic reform and we should finish the job that Holt started and Malcolm Fraser built upon with his land rights laws. Even we, the Liberal Party, think of his disappearance more than we do his considerable historical achievement of the 1967 referendum. As this book chronicles, the Liberal Party has a history of Indigenous affairs which has been both good and bad. Holt set the ball rolling. Sadly, his legacy has been distorted because of his untimely and unusual death. It is my hope that this book can be part of a Holt revival. Holt delivered a significant constitutional reform with the biggest margin of any referendum in Australian history. It is also apparent that the name Bill Wentworth should be better known. Wentworth was a pioneer of both the 1967 referendum and the land rights agenda. He was a radical liberal in his day. Yet he was otherwise extremely conservative on social matters relating to women and sexuality.

Malcolm Fraser delivered land rights in 1976. This system along with other land schemes like native title have resulted in more than half of Australia being handed back to Indigenous people. Yet there were periods in the Menzies and Howard eras when more could have been done; both differently and better. Menzies probably should have moved on the referendum before retiring and Howard should have offered a formal apology before Kevin Rudd did so in 2008.

We should have converted the 1999 Sydney Harbour Bridge

walk for reconciliation into an apology. Australia has come a long way in my thirty-six years of life. Who could forget the howls of protest when a Burri Gubbi woman from central Queensland, Cathy Freeman, pulled out both the Aboriginal and Australian flags in Victoria, Canada at the 1994 Commonwealth Games. When Freeman brandished both flags at the Sydney Olympics, it was perhaps the most unifying moment in Australian history. As a sixteen-year-old, I stood at Circular Quay watching on the big screen, about a hundred metres from where I would open my electorate office nineteen years later.

On the personnel front, the Liberal Party has delivered the firsts: the first Indigenous member of federal parliament in Senator Neville Bonner, from the Jugarah people in southeast Queensland, and the first Indigenous cabinet minister in Ken Wyatt MP, who belongs to the Noongar in southwest and Yamatji in midwest Western Australia, is also the first Aboriginal person to serve as Minister for Indigenous Australians. But we in the Liberal Party have not engaged as widely in the Indigenous debates as our Labor colleagues.

A cursory view of the history in this field shows that we have failed to claim our own contribution to history. How many Australians know about Harold Holt's leadership in delivering the 1967 referendum? Very few. There are a few pages about Holt's 1967 triumph in Geoffrey Blainey's history book, *The Australian People*, and a few more in Tom Frame's biography of Holt. That's it. Too many Australians think that modern Australia started in 1972 when the Whitlam government was elected. I appreciate John Howard's discussion of how Menzies created modern Australia, especially *The Menzies Era*. I worry, however, that the lack of historical documentation and recognition has discouraged those in the Liberal Party from engaging in Indigenous policy—a development that is detrimental to all of us. It has reduced the size of the canvas upon which we work in Canberra in the present.

Former prime minister Tony Abbott bemoaned the lack of books written by Liberal Party MPs. He said, "the relative scarcity of books from the conservative side of politics by Liberal and National Party politicians could prompt the conclusion that we have little worth saying." Like Abbott, I have found that writing longform pieces whilst in public office helps develop and articulate the thoughts necessary to be a productive advocate. In this book, I hope to rebalance history by reminding others in the Liberal Party about the contribution of Australian liberalism, the good and the bad. I hope this will encourage people in the Liberal Party to be more ambitious when it comes to reconciliation.

1

Bugiya Yesterday— remembering our history

THIS BOOK DOES not seek to run through all the details of the past 250 years of modern Australian history. Rather, it seeks to cover the history of Indigenous advocacy and the Liberal Party during the period of significant cultural, political, and legal change which commenced in the 1960s. This history is concerned with national politics from the 1960s, when the Commonwealth government assumed responsibility for Indigenous affairs.

The developments from the 1960s onward do show the disastrous shortcomings of discriminatory and then paternalistic policy. But they also show both a history of resilience of the Indigenous people and a history of meaningful constitutional and legal changes—

many at the hands of Liberal governments. Alas, there has been no narrative on the Liberal Party's record on Indigenous affairs, and so its history of positive incremental changes is easily forgotten. This failure curtails the ability to propose new positive changes in the present and the future.

1770–1900—the colonial era

For historical context, the problem began in 1770 with two Latin words. *Terra nullius*. Land belonging to no one. It was a spear through the heart of 60,000 years of Indigenous inhabitation. James Cook raised the British flag at Possession Island off the tip of Cape York Peninsula and claimed possession of the whole east coast of Australia in the name of the British Crown. He did so not by treaty with or conquest of the Indigenous populations but on the basis that the land was *terra nullius*. In effect, *terra nullius* implies that Australia belonged to no one because Indigenous Australians were thought to have no concept of law or property ownership, and so no rights to the land. Almost two decades later, in 1788, the British occupation of the settlement of New South Wales began under the governorship of Arthur Philip in Sydney. King George III gave instructions to Philip to treat Aboriginal people with "amity and kindness" in adherence with a duty of protection and education. Most estimates put the Indigenous population across the continent at the time at 750,000; they became British subjects of the British Crown.

The second settlement after New South Wales was established on the southern island known as Van Diemen's Land, which is today's Tasmania. One historian of Tasmania's Aboriginal people, Cassandra Pybus, recounts how dispossession was genuinely bewildering to the Indigenous people who found that their access to their own land was restrained or prohibited: "the original owners would not leave, the colonial secretary complained because they were 'possessed with the idea of their own rights over the country in comparison with the colonists'."[1] The taking of the land without compensation set the course for centuries of dispute.

There was great resistance in many places and clashes were reported over the next ten years in the Parramatta and Hawkesbury districts. In places like Camp Cove and Double Bay in Sydney, Aboriginal people lived in and around the new settlements in relative harmony, but without effective legal equality.[2] In other parts of the Australian colonies, notably in Van Diemen's Land (Tasmania), there were policies like the Black Line which forced the removal and near extermination of the Aboriginal population. The late 1800s were characterized by wholesale dispossession of Aboriginal people through disease and violence, as the frontier of British settlement expanded. Throughout the nineteenth century, some individuals, colonial officials, and governments recognised that Aboriginal people did have organized societies and possessed property rights which should be recognised or compensated in some way. But there was no redress.

Beyond the dispossession of land without consent, the British settlement of the Australian colonies was also a humanitarian disaster. There was anxiety about it in London during the colonial period. Protection boards designed to protect the Aboriginal communities in most Australian colonies were established. The paternalistic efforts to 'protect' the Aboriginal population often achieved the opposite result. The humanitarian disaster in Van Diemen's Land resulted in the loss of so much life that a Nuenonne or Bruny Island woman known as Truganini was widely flagged as the 'last Tasmanian Aboriginal' when she died in 1876. Truganini was not the last Aboriginal, primarily thanks to the sealing industry which was concentrated around Tasmanian islands. The sealers (settlers) would establish families in remote islands with Tasmanian Aboriginal people, ensuring they were safe from the colonial authorities in Hobart.

There was one well-documented attempt at a 'treaty' from a Tasmanian explorer, John Batman, who likely participated in massacres in Tasmania as part of the murderous Black Line policy. In Victoria, as a representative of the Port Phillip (Victoria) Association, Batman entered into an agreement with the Aboriginal people in the Port Phillip area in 1835. It was the first documented land-use agreement that sought to recognise pre-existing Aboriginal rights to land. His negotiations with local Indigenous leaders led to a contract to buy their land in exchange for blankets and trinkets and the like. But Batman's 'treaty' was declared invalid by Governor Bourke of New South Wales on the basis that the British Crown owned the entire New South Wales colony (at that time including the whole east coast), and that only it could sell or distribute 'vacant' land. So Batman could not buy land from the Indigenous leaders because it was not legally theirs to sell.

With the sovereignty of the British Crown, all Aboriginal people became British subjects and the original colonial constitutions (granted by the Imperial Parliament at Westminster) granted manhood suffrage to all resident British subjects—including Aboriginals. Two colonies reacted against this—Queensland disenfranchised Aboriginal people under the *Elections Act 1885* (repeated in the *Elections Acts Amendment Act 1905*), and Western

Australia did likewise under the *Constitution Acts Amendment Act 1893* (repeated by the *Western Australia Electoral Act 1907*). In the other colonies, Aboriginal people could generally enrol to vote. The net result of the colonial period was widespread dispossession as well as disease and a much smaller Aboriginal population.

1901—federated Australia

Australia was constituted as a nation in 1901. The new nation excluded Indigenous people from certain civic activities and the nation's birth certificate went out of its way to do so but it was incongruent from the outset. For example, Indigenous people were British subjects but not to be counted in the census. The Australian Constitution originally stated that Aboriginal people will not be counted in the census, and that the Commonwealth has the power to make laws relating to any race of people in Australia with the exception of Aboriginals.

In 1902, the *Commonwealth Franchise Act*, denied the voting rights of "Aboriginal natives of Australia . . . unless so entitled under section 41 of the Constitution", that is, unless they were already enrolled to vote in State elections. In many cases, Aboriginal people were entitled to vote in colonial and then State elections. In New South Wales, Victoria, South Australia, and Tasmania, Aboriginal people could vote in certain circumstances. More Aboriginal people were granted the right to vote in 1949, when the *Commonwealth Electoral Act 1949* provided the franchise to any Aboriginal person who had served in the defence forces.

Indigenous groups began to get organized from the 1920s. The Australian Aboriginal Progressive Association was founded by

Fred Maynard, a Wonnarua man from the upper Hunter Valley in New South Wales, who was an activist and rights campaigner. It operated between 1924 and 1929, and was the first recorded politically organized Aboriginal activist group. It held rallies, conducted meetings, wrote letters and petitions to the government and to King George V about the injustice and inequality forced upon Aboriginal people. A focus of particular attention was the New South Wales Aboriginal Protection Board's child removal and land confiscation policies. The Association's demands focused both on land rights and civil rights, including full voting rights and the replacement of the Aboriginal Protection Board by an all-Aboriginal board. In 1927, two Wiradjuri elders from central New South Wales, Jimmy Clements (also known as 'King Billy') and John Noble (also known as 'Marvellous'), walked more than 150 kilometres to attend the opening ceremony at Parliament House in the presence of the Duke and Duchess of York. They walked to Canberra to claim their "sovereign rights to the Federal Capital Territory" at the very moment the sovereignty of the Crown and the Australian Parliament was asserted.

The Australian Aboriginal Progressive Association made a submission to the 1927-29 Royal Commission on the Australian Constitution arguing for the federalisation of Aboriginal affairs and protesting against child removal, land theft, and abuse of Aboriginal people by police and boards of protection. The Commission received many submissions from feminist, anti-slavery, and other humanitarian groups stressing the exploitation and dispossession of Aboriginal people, how this reflected on Australia's international standing in the British Commonwealth League, and the need to make Aboriginal people a federal government responsibility, in order to eliminate 'parochial' State interests from contributing to their exploitation. Several witnesses even took up the suggestion for a new Aboriginal State to be established in Arnhem Land. The demands were heard, but rejected.

The majority report of the 1927 Royal Commission into the Constitution rejected calls for a constitutional amendment, noting "the effect of the treatment of Aboriginals on the reputation of Australia furnishes a powerful argument for a transference of control to the Commonwealth" but recommended that "on the whole the states are better equipped for controlling Aboriginals than the Commonwealth". The report said the national parliament "should see that all carried their fair share of burden in respect to the displaced native races, and should accept responsibility for their well-being". In response to the Commission, Fred Maynard called for an Aboriginal representative in the federal parliament, or failing that, for an Aboriginal Ambassador to be appointed, who would live in Canberra, watch over his people's interests, and advise the federal authorities.

Not to put too fine a point on it, but this was probably the first attempt to provide a Voice to Parliament. Meanwhile, there was an open wound which to this day still hasn't healed. A Day of Mourning was declared on 26 January 1938 by Aboriginal activists led by William Ferguson of the Warangesda Mission at the Murrumbidgee Riverina in western New South Wales, Jack Patten of the Cummeragunja Reserve on the border between New South Wales and Victoria, and Pearl Gibbs, a Ngemba woman of the Barwon Darling region in New South Wales. Together they organized a Day of Mourning conference in Sydney. The conference was open only to Aboriginals and the following resolution was passed:

We, representing the Aboriginals of Australia, assembled in conference at the Australia Hall, Sydney, on the 26th day of January, 1938, this being the 150th anniversary of the Whiteman's seizure of our country, hereby make protest against the callous treatment of our people by the Whiteman during the past 150 years, and we appeal to the Australian nation of today to make new laws for the education and care of Aboriginals, and we ask for a new policy which will raise our people to full citizen status and equality within the community.

The resolution and speeches stressed the need for full citizenship rights for all Aboriginal people, that degree of descent or fairness of skin should not dictate access to rights, that the Commonwealth should have greater control over Aboriginal affairs and that Aboriginals should be involved in policy decisions and their implementation. A ten-point plan based on resolutions from the Day of Mourning conference was presented by a deputation of Aboriginals to the prime minister, Joseph Lyons.

Constitution-related activism from the 1930s mainly focused on advocating for constitutional change to promote legal equality and to give the Commonwealth powers to legislate for Aboriginal people, rather than on treaties or distinct representative bodies. The Curtin government put forward a referendum to transfer fourteen constitutional powers, most of which were economic in nature. One included a proposal on "including the rehabilitation of ex-servicemen, national health, family allowances and 'the people of the Aboriginal race'", from the States to the Commonwealth for a period of five years after the conclusion of the Second World War in order to assist post-war reconstruction.

While the opposition United Australia Party was generally in favour of the transfer of powers to legislate for Aboriginal people, they opposed most of the other transfers. The referendum was framed as a single question on all fourteen powers and so the issue of Aboriginal legislation could not be separated from the others. The referendum failed, only achieving a majority vote in Western Australia and South Australia. The defeat of the referendum left the States to run Indigenous policy. But there was also resilience and strength. The communities endured and became powerful advocates.

The Menzies era

The last five years of the Menzies era were heady. There was progress: voting rights were passed, and a national Indigenous heritage protection organization was established. There was extensive debate over constitutional exclusion and the Bark Petitions were presented in 1963. The Yolngu people developed these petitions in English and Gumatj to proclaim their ownership of the land around Melville Bay in the Northern Territory. In the translation of the first traditional document recognised by the parliament, the Yolngu people said "that the people of this area fear that their needs and interests will be completely ignored as they have been ignored in the past."[3] The petitions were sent to a committee of inquiry which made recommendations that were not adopted by the government.

In 1962, the Menzies government amended the *Commonwealth Electoral Act* by giving the vote to all Aboriginal people in Commonwealth and Northern Territory elections. Prior to 1962, the federal franchise for Aboriginals extended to those past and present members of the defence forces, those compulsorily enrolled in Victoria, those voluntarily enrolled in New South Wales and South Australia and the 'non-native' Aboriginal people of Queensland

and Western Australia. In his 1962 Second Reading Speech, the Minister for Territories, Paul Hasluck, said, "The path of reform is not to give [Aboriginals] something that they did not previously have; the path of reform is to take away the disability that the various colonial and State parliaments have imposed on them."[4] Paul Hasluck dedicated a large part of his career to Aboriginal studies and he argued for full legal equality in his 1940s master's thesis. It is perhaps unsurprising that Hasluck was the minister who carried voting rights legislation through the Menzies government which guaranteed the right to vote in federal elections from 1962.

In 1965, Menzies introduced two Constitution Alteration Bills. Section 24 of the Constitution stated that the number of members of the House of Representatives should be "as nearly as practicable twice the number of the Senators". The government wanted to break the nexus between the numbers in the two houses. The Constitution Alteration (Parliament) Bill would have provided for an enlarged House of Representatives to provide smaller constituencies whilst keeping the Senate proportionally smaller. The other was the Constitution Alteration (Repeal of Section 127) Bill. This section excluded Indigenous people from the census. Menzies described section 127 as being "completely out of harmony with our national attitudes". It was out of harmony with the attitudes of the 1960s, it was also most likely out of harmony with the directives from London to treat Indigenous people with respect in an earlier era.

The prime minister used his first reading speech to explain why he was not including an amendment of section 51(xxvi) which would give the Commonwealth power to legislate for Aboriginal people. Menzies argued that the words "other than the Aboriginal race in any State" was a protection *against* discrimination by the

Commonwealth Parliament. He held that if the phrase was removed, the parliament could set up "a separate body of industrial, social, criminal and other laws relating exclusively to Aboriginals". Menzies's point seems academic and did not resonate with the debate taking place in Australia and the United States on rights. This policy allowed the States to maintain their control over Indigenous affairs which in some jurisdictions like Queensland and Western Australia was simply appalling. The possibility he outlined seemed unthinkable as it would leave the Commonwealth without any capacity and the exclusionary words intact. Regardless, the Bill was passed and a date was set for a referendum.

The retirement of Menzies early in January 1966, after more than eighteen years as prime minister, provided a new political environment in which to debate the matter. It is perhaps ironic that for thirty-five years of the twentieth century an Aboriginal man, Alf Stafford of the Gamilaroi in northern New South Wales and southern Queensland and the Darug in western Sydney, worked closely with eleven prime ministers and became a friend and confidant to Sir Robert Menzies. Until his retirement in 1972, Stafford was a driver for prime ministers and opposition leaders. He was one of twelve children born in Binnaway in New South Wales, and took the job after being discharged from the Australian Army. He was also an accomplished cricketer.

Given his service to prime ministers from Lyons to Whitlam, it's curious that his presence at the epicentre of Australian politics is largely unrecognised. So close was he to Menzies that he became a selector for the PM's XI cricket team. When Stafford's wife, Edith, became ill with cancer in the 1950s, Menzies realised that Stafford's driving responsibilities were keeping Alf from his family. He fashioned a new role for Stafford as Cabinet Officer, which effectively made him a personal assistant. After Stafford's wife died, Menzies insisted that he reside at The Lodge to better support his children.

In 1956, Stafford went on to marry one of Menzies's housekeepers, and Sir Robert and Dame Pattie threw a wedding reception for the couple at The Lodge. Menzies even asked him to sit in for him when renowned portrait painter Sir William Dargie composed a portrait in 1963. It prompted this quote from author Paul Daley in 2016: "This incident entices so many metaphors: of the Indigenous heart that beats, too often undetected and unacknowledged, at the core of national identity; of sovereignty's black core defying the white face; of the capacity for symbiosis between men with ostensibly little in common."[5]

Towards the end of his long period in office, Menzies established the Australian Institute of Aboriginal Studies (later known as AIATSIS) at the urging of his colleague, Bill Wentworth. AIATSIS is an amazing resource of language and culture. Wentworth said in his Second Reading speech, "We are preserving the linguistics, the semantics, the material for art studies, for studies and material culture, of the nature of authority and indeed the nature of man. What is available for study here cannot be studied anywhere else. It can only be studied in Australia, now."[6] Sadly, no prime minister visited AIATSIS until Malcolm Turnbull in 2017. It is to the great credit of the Menzies government that it created AIATSIS because it wanted to conserve Indigenous heritage, language, and culture; a natural instinct for a conservative government.

Holt government

Harold Holt became prime minister on Australia Day 1966. He led the most successful referendum in Australian history—90.7% of Australians voted in favour of two changes to the Constitution. Holt is remembered as the prime minister lost at sea. He should be remembered as the prime minister of Australia who delivered an historic reform. His only biographer, Professor Tom Frame, sets out how Holt was determined for constitutional change upon his ascension. In his lengthy assessment of Holt's life, Frame devotes only four pages to the referendum. That is four pages in the only Holt biography which deals with the historic referendum. This compares unfavorably to the reams of paper which exist on Gough Whitlam and Aboriginal affairs. This is perhaps the best and worst example of the failure of Australian liberalism to document and venerate core achievements throughout modern Australian history.

On 27 May 1967, the referendum cleared the way for the national government to make laws for Aboriginal people and removed section 127 which excluded Aboriginal people from being counted in the census of the Australian population. In doing so, it removed both references to Aboriginal people in the Australian Constitution. Holt gave effect to the advocacy of the Aboriginal leadership, who psephologist and commentator Malcolm Mackerras has said "were becoming determined that the Commonwealth be given a concurrent power to make laws with respect to the people of the Aboriginal race."[7] The Commonwealth's expanded race power emerged from the removal of the words "other than the Aboriginal race in any State". The change had been rejected by the Menzies government, which had solely wanted to remove section 127 of the Constitution because it excluded Aboriginals from official census counts.

Menzies casts a heavy shadow over Holt in Australian political history. This is a great shame because of this significant achievement of Holt's administration. But as the leadership change approached, there was unrest and political organization. The Freedom Rides throughout western New South Wales had occurred in 1965. Led by Aboriginal activist Charles Perkins (whose central Australian ancestors were Arrernte and Kalkadoon from the Mount Isa region of Queensland), a group of Sydney University students named Student Action for Aboriginals hired a bus and drove through towns like Walgett.

The clear purpose was to highlight the segregation and racism that was occurring away from the lights of the big cities. Perkins based the concept on the activities in the 1960s of the American civil rights movement. Perkins wrote in his biography that the Walgett people were shell-shocked when the bus turned up:

> We took our banners and posters and stood in front of the Walgett RSL. That was in the morning at about eleven o'clock. The heat was tremendous as it was summer-time . . . They had never seen anything like it in their lives. People stared. It was a completely new experience, like seeing television for the first time or seeing a moonship fly past their window. Walgett people could not believe it was happening in Walgett. A protest on behalf of the town niggers!

The media covered the events and the pressure continued to build. The assessment of Perkins's Indigenous contemporary and fellow activist John Moriarty, a Yanyuwa man from the southern region of the Gulf of Carpentaria, sums up Perkins's achievement: "I thought Charlie did a really good job with it. He did a great job of bringing attention to the plight of Aboriginals to the rest of Australia, it really got a lot of press. It gave the rest of Australia a much greater awareness about our struggle for equality especially leading up to the referendum."[8]

The ask

Groups like the Aboriginal Progressive Association had, for many years, argued that a federal power was required because the States were not up to the job. The Freedom Rides appeared to have reinforced the sense that the States would not move fast enough or even adequately. Indeed, the Commonwealth had regularly used the argument that it didn't have sufficient authority to deal with Aboriginal affairs. This was the position of both the Lyons and Curtin governments. As mentioned, the Curtin government included the power to deal with Aboriginal affairs as part of its 'fourteen powers' referendum which was defeated.

The Federal Council for the Advancement of Aboriginals was established in 1958 in Adelaide to lead lobbying on questions of citizenship and belonging to the Australian nation. In 1962, the Council ran a national petition which set out an anti-discrimination agenda. 1962 is the year that the Menzies government delivered voting rights to Indigenous Australians. The Council's agenda was rightly ambitious and sought to eliminate discrimination through federal supremacy. There were two changes sought. Firstly, the Council said, "The Federal Parliament must get the authority to pass uniform laws that would override the existing state laws"— this involves changing section 51. But the Council also recognised that changes would be needed at a "referendum to amend the Constitution so that these clauses which discriminate against

Aboriginals can be removed."[9] In effect, they were seeking the federal government first to acquire power and then to exercise it to stop discrimination.

The issues of discrimination were set out in a 1962 brochure which identified issues like free movement, award wages, property ownership, state voting rights, and alcohol consumption as matters which could be solved through a new federal power.

The Council said, "The only practical way in which these variations can be removed is for the Commonwealth to possess and exercise the power to make laws with respect to Aboriginals." The second amendment sought to remove section 127 which "excludes Aboriginals from these people counted in the Census. The Government considers cattle, sheep and pigs important enough to be counted officially but not the Aboriginal people."[10] The Council argued there were both moral and practical reasons for removing section 127.

Despite being allowed to vote at federal elections, Aboriginal people could not be counted in the census. The Council said, "Aboriginals may now vote at federal elections but are not counted in the census which is used to fix electoral boundaries. The exercising of this right will increase the size of the electorate and so decrease the effectiveness of their vote. Both Queensland and Western Australia probably lost a seat in the House of Representatives because of this section." Back in 1965, the Menzies cabinet considered submissions from the Attorney-General, Bill Snedden, on constitutional matters. Snedden's 1965 cabinet submission argued for the abolition of section 127 so that Aboriginals can be "recognised as forming part of the population of their State for the purposes of the Commonwealth Constitution." He cited practical reasons and our international reputation in making his case.[11]

On the question of section 51, Snedden said he does "not personally accept that in truth (section 51 was discriminatory)". But he goes on to say that the national government should have the capacity to legislate for Aboriginal people. Snedden said:

> I think also that the average elector would feel that either the Commonwealth should have the power in section 51 in relation to all races, including people of the Aboriginal race, or ought not to have the power at all; and I believe that failure to include a proposal to delete the underlined words might well prejudice the success of a referendum that sought the repeal of section 127.

This submission of 22 February 1965 was partly endorsed by the Menzies cabinet, which agreed to remove section 127 but proposed leaving section 51 as it was. The Menzies position would therefore meet half of the Aboriginal groups' requests. The Menzies position was to leave the Constitution with one reference to race. This position did not last the summer.

Holt's referendum process

Upon coming to power on Australia Day 1967, Holt got to work. On 15 February he said he was reviewing the Menzies referenda proposals:

> We see ahead of us a crowded and unusually active political year. We feel that, in addition to performing an increasing volume of administrative tasks, we should, as a new Government, make a thorough review of current policies. In the swiftly-moving world of today, some changes may well appear to us to have become desirable.[12]

He put the Menzies referendum on hold and established a new cabinet discussion on the matter. Holt's press secretary at the time,

Tony Eggleton, recalls:

> The need for action in respect of the Aboriginal community was being strongly and effectively promoted but, initially, Harold and many of his cabinet colleagues were cautious and sometimes ambivalent. He did not express public concern but, privately, reflected on the difficulty of overcoming public antipathy to constitutional reform. The prime minister began expanding his contact with Aboriginal representatives and assessing the federal initiatives that would be of most value to the Aboriginal people.[13]

A cabinet submission of 22 February 1967 set out the view of the new Attorney-General, Nigel Bowen: "I am myself firmly of the belief that there would be a large area of dissatisfaction with the Commonwealth if it does nothing about section 51."[14] It was noted in his submission that any attempt to establish a Commonwealth power would be resisted by some States—thereby complicating the referendum which would otherwise have been simpler under the Menzies model. Bowen summarised his advice as follows: "moreover, I think that any step to remove from the Constitution words alleged to be discriminatory against the Aboriginal people would be welcomed by a very large section of the Australian people."[15] The Holt cabinet agreed and the ambition of the change doubled.

The Holt position

On 23 February 1967, Holt told the House of Representatives that the government had a new policy:

> The Government has decided to propose that the words "other than the Aboriginal race" in any State be omitted from the section. While the original intention in inserting these words was to safeguard the position of people of the Aboriginal race they have been widely misinterpreted and there is a general impression that they are

discriminatory.

This suggested that the Commonwealth would be seeking power to overrule the States if need be on Aboriginal affairs. As Ian Sinclair, a Menzies and Holt era minister, recalls, "The view was that the States thought they were doing the right thing but it didn't always work out that way." Legislation was introduced in March 1967 in which Holt addressed directly in the House: "I am glad to say that no vote was cast against the proposals relating to Aboriginals. In all the circumstances, the Government has decided that the referendum should be held on 27th of May 1967."

In a media release issued two weeks before the referendum, Holt said, "It is completely out of harmony with our national attitudes and modern thinking. It has no place in our Constitution in this age." There were few other public statements in the lead up to the vote on 27 May. The ironic referendum jingle was "vote yes for Aboriginals, they want to be Australians too." On the day after the referendum, Holt said at Kingsford Smith airport:

I think we can all as a nation take satisfaction in the overwhelming support given to the proposal to remove any trace of discrimination, as it has appeared to many people, in the Australian Constitution. It will not only be of benefit—as I see it—to people of the Aboriginal race in that it will enable the national government to cooperate more closely with the Governments of the States in ensuring just treatment and full acceptance in the Australian community of the Aboriginal people, but I think it will help Australia's image abroad in that so many Australians have shown their determination to give full acceptance to people of the Aboriginal race in the Australian community.[16]

It has been noted by some commentators that Holt did not campaign strongly in favour of the change. Frame says, "Holt was deeply distressed by the need for the referendum. As a former immigration Minister who had welcomed people of many different nationalities to this country, he was not convinced that Australia had the serious race problems he had observed elsewhere."

This would not be an uncommon perspective of the time. Yet the record shows that Holt, not Menzies, put the full suite of constitutional changes sought by the Aboriginal leadership on the table, urged a yes vote and delivered the yes majority. So why did Holt do it? His contemporary H. C. 'Nugget' Coombs, who was the first Governor of the Reserve Bank, wrote that initiatives in the arts and Aboriginal policy space "better expressed his own generous and human spirit." This is backed up by Ian Sinclair, the last of the Menzies/Holt-era ministers, who recalls, "Holt had a strong social conscience, he was very concerned about Indigenous people and he tried to help them. Holt wanted to break away from the traditional approach of Menzies. He was much more sympathetic."[17] Another contemporary journalist Edgar Holt says Harold was perhaps the "nicest man Australia had as a Prime Minister."

Eggleton recollects:

> Harold was determined to do more for Aboriginals. The referendum was to give a better deal for Aboriginals. In his two years as prime minister he set out to further extend his first-hand knowledge of Indigenous issues. While on a mission to New York, Harold took keen interest in an Aboriginal delegation visiting the United States. He asked me to arrange for Charles Perkins and his colleagues to call on him at the Waldorf Astoria Hotel. I had the pleasure of escorting the visitors to the PM's suite and, after the meeting, it was evident that Harold's focus on Indigenous issues had been further sharpened. He began looking in more detail at ways in which the federal government could most positively move forward. There were visits to Aboriginal communities and Aboriginal leaders (including with Charles Perkins).[18]

Bill Wentworth

Bill Wentworth was a backbencher during the Holt premiership, so it is hard to ascertain his direct impact on Holt. However, his influence in Aboriginal affairs can be traced back to 1952, when he made a ministerial statement in parliament on 'native welfare'. As with the American President, Lyndon Johnson's influence on Holt, Wentworth's influence appears to have been a factor in shaping Holt's approach to Indigenous affairs. There is no doubting Wentworth's commitment. In March 1966, Wentworth introduced a private member's bill for a Constitution alteration to delete section 51(xxvi) and create a new section which would prevent discrimination against anyone "within the Commonwealth by reason of his racial origin."

Ian Sinclair, Holt's social services minister, vividly recalls Wentworth's influence: "The work Wentworth did was outstanding—he recorded dying languages so they could be used in future. He did it across the many different people, different Aboriginal nations."[19] AIATSIS does exactly what Wentworth hoped: language, art, culture, and practice has been conserved and, in some cases, reborn. It is thanks to AIATSIS that the word buraadja—the title of this book—has been preserved. It is from the Dhurga language of the Yuin nation on the southeast coast of New South Wales. In July 2020, certain Yuin traditional owners along with AIATSIS published a dictionary of the language, which ensures it will live on. Credit must go to the three co-authors, Waine Donovan, Patricia Ellis and Kerry Boyenga, who created the Dhurga dictionary. Bringing a language like Dhurga back to life is an immeasurable achievement and as the title of this book demonstrates, it can find a new life in contemporary Australia.

Apart from successfully agitating to have AIATSIS established, Wentworth was active on all things Indigenous. He had a passion for Indigenous culture throughout his long parliamentary career. As late as 1976, he was speaking on Aboriginal land rights legislation, and arguing in favour of bilingual education and the use of Aboriginal languages in schools. Philip Ruddock, who served in parliament with Wentworth, recalls, "Billy was a fascinating character. He used to go out every year to just bond with Indigenous people. In recess, he would just pack up in his four-wheel drive and go." Wentworth became the first minister appointed to the role of Aboriginal affairs in February 1968, in which office he served until May 1971 in the First and Second Gorton Ministries. Eggleton regards Wentworth as an influencer: "There were influences and Harold appreciated advice. Billy Wentworth contributed much, and especially Barrie Dexter." Barrie Dexter was a diplomat and the first Secretary of the Department of Aboriginal Affairs.

A more direct influence on Holt was Lyndon Johnson. Eggleton says of President Johnson (LBJ): "Often, when Harold was with LBJ, there was discussion about civil rights. LBJ took us to various places to talk about the Great Society and the War on Poverty." Holt's grandson, Robert Holt, speaks to the family story on the influence of President Johnson:

> My Grandmother [Zara Holt], whom I was very close to, would often talk about the close friendship between President Johnson and Harold. She told me that they thought the same way on many matters. Harold was particularly inspired by the story of Johnson's determination to act on civil rights based on his experience as a young schoolteacher on the Texas/Mexican border in El Paso. He described how, when teaching these bright young students, their bright eyes would literally dim at the realisation that the world of American opportunity was not open to them. She said that Harold

would often question Johnson on his civil rights agenda and his challenges in Congress. She also told me that Johnson would ask Harold detailed questions about the plight of Australia's Indigenous population.[20]

There is no doubt about the closeness of the relationship between Holt and Johnson, who delivered a most substantial civil rights agenda including the 1964 Civil Rights Act and voting reform. Holt's disappearance on 17 December 1967 devastated Johnson. The journalist, author, and historian, Troy Bramston, described the intense emotion of Johnson's visit to Australia for Holt's memorial service:

> Before the memorial service at St Paul's Cathedral in Melbourne on December 22, Johnson visited Zara Holt at her home in Toorak. Eggleton escorted Johnson inside. The President and the Prime Minister's widow bonded in their grief. And they wept.[21]

In his own words, Johnson was clear about his loss:

> My personal loss is heavy. He and the people for whom he spoke were always dependable and unshakable. Those blessings of his example cannot be removed. They are as eternal as the sea that has taken this good and gallant champion away.[22]

Holt's Attorney-General, Nigel Bowen, does not appear to be an influencer on Indigenous issues. His singular contribution on Aboriginal affairs dealt with the inclusion of Aboriginals in the census as part of the debate on the Constitution amendment bill of 1967.

Response to the referendum

The response to the 1967 referendum result from the Aboriginal groups was naturally very positive. The Federal Council for the Advancement of Aboriginals wrote to Holt on 29 May saying, "Congratulations on a job well done on the referendum Yes vote for Aboriginal rights . . . undoubtedly the people of Australia also favour a better deal for Aboriginals as shown by the result of the vote."[23] Eggleton recalls:

> Harold was surprised and pleased at the degree of support, and began looking in more detail at ways in which the federal government could most constructively and move positively forward Indigenous issues and to expand his personal appreciation of Aboriginal history, culture, and aspirations. There were visits to Aboriginal communities and more consultations with Indigenous leaders.[24]

As a concrete step, Holt established a Council for Aboriginal Affairs and decided to take direct responsibility by placing the Office of Aboriginal Affairs in his own Department. Eggleton says, "Over a period of just a few months, Harold Holt had come a long way in crystallising his thinking on Aboriginal policies and in his personal commitment."

Neville Bonner

Holt's referendum drove one Neville Bonner into politics—the first Indigenous member of federal parliament. Bonner's first political engagement was handing out How to Vote cards during the 1967 referendum. On referendum day, Bonner handed out the cards at a polling booth, and there he was approached by Labor MP Bill Hayden, who is alleged to have said, "Aren't you working for the wrong team? You should be giving out cards for us?"[25] Bonner told biographer Angela Berger that "It browned me off with the ALP thinking, the assumption that Aboriginals should automatically belong to that party."[26] And so it was that on 22 August 1967, Neville Bonner joined the Old Mile branch of the Liberal Party (Queensland Division). Over the next two years, he worked his way into the inner sanctum of the Queensland Division.

Bonner said of his agenda in 1970, "I felt it important for the race to get an Aboriginal into Parliament and saw that maybe I was the only one at that time who would have a chance."[27] As a liberal-conservative, Bonner set out his unifying credentials and his concern for his own people. In his preselection speech, he said, "Let me make it clear, I seek to go to Canberra to advance the whole of the Australian nation and its people rather than to advance the cause of a part."[28]

Then in his maiden speech, he said, "Less than 200 years ago came the white man. My people were shot, poisoned, hanged, broken in spirit. They became refugees in their own land. But it is history and we take care now of the present and look to the future." He added, "Too long, too long we have been crying out and far too few have heeded our calling." Bonner did a good deal on environmental issues in his time, especially on ensuring certain mining projects did not proceed. Ian Viner, the minister responsible for Malcolm Fraser's groundbreaking land rights laws of 1976, credits Bonner as being crucial to the Senate voting in favour.[29]

A new Commonwealth power

Following the referendum, Holt said the result "will contribute to Australia's international standing by demonstrating to the outside world our overwhelming desire to give full acceptance to the Aboriginal people within our community."[30] The great value in having a Commonwealth power meant that laws could later be made on significant issues—land rights, native title, and heritage protection. There are another eighteen acts of parliament on the federal statute books which would not exist without the Commonwealth's power secured under Holt.

The reality is that Holt's constitutional amendments led to a strong new power for the national government which it has relied upon for significant reforms. The High Court has found that federal laws such as the *World Heritage Properties Conservation Act 1983* and *Native Title Act 1993* were supported by the Holt amendments to section 51, as are numerous other laws enacted by the national parliament reliant upon the 1967 amendments.[31]

Holt went on to engage deeply with Indigenous communities. 'Nugget' Coombs would chair the new Council for Aboriginal Affairs, alongside former diplomat Barrie Dexter and ANU academic Bill Stanner—the man who would coin the Great Australian Silence as a reflection of the imbalance in our history. The three-person committee was established on 2 November 1967. Coombs said, "[Holt] assured me that it was his firm intention to use the new Commonwealth powers genuinely to transform the status and welfare of Aboriginals and his actions gave evidence of his sincerity in that undertaking."[32] To demonstrate his commitment to Aboriginal causes, Holt established the administrative base in his own department. Eggleton recalls, "In the second half of 1967, Harold sought the advice of the likes of Coombs, Barrie Dexter and Bill Wentworth. In planning the Government's programmes for 1968, Indigenous affairs was moving up a list of domestic priorities." Sadly, it was not to be for Holt, who perished on 17 December 1967. Eggleton said it was on Holt's mind as he went for the fateful swim:

> Harold rang me from Portsea on the morning of Saturday 16 December to confirm arrangements for a news conference to be held

in Melbourne the following week. He would use this as a forum to reflect on the past year and to outline his agenda for 1968. Harold's accidental drowning meant that it was left to others to build on the opportunities flowing from the referendum.[33]

Barrie Dexter said with regret:

Prime Minister Holt assured Coombs that high priority was to be given to the advancement of Aboriginal Australians and that the Council for Aboriginal Affairs would be set up either by statute or by charter from the Prime Minister himself, with executive powers to investigate, to consult, and to make recommendations to the Prime Minister and Government. However, following Holt's death in December 1967, Stanner later commented that this "particular conception of the Council . . . died with him . . . There was never any basic document that covered the Council's existence and task" and the Council remained a 'de facto' rather than 'formal' body.

Post-Holt years

John Gorton became the first prime minister to sit in the Senate when he succeeded Harold Holt. Sinclair recalls, "Gorton's interest in Aboriginal affairs was limited." This accords with Gorton's limited public statements and authorised biography, in which he claims to be committed to assimilation rather than to self-determination. On his first day as prime minister, the Gorton government "presaged a greater Commonwealth involvement in Aboriginal affairs . . . by considering ways whereby Aboriginal citizens could choose their own representatives to advise the Council for Aboriginal Affairs and [Billy] Wentworth's office."[34]

There is a continuous tradition in the Liberal Party from Holt to Wentworth to Fraser. Gorton appointed Billy Wentworth as the first Minister for Aboriginal Affairs. Wentworth used this position to argue for land for Aboriginals. His staffer (and later Senator for

New South Wales) Chris Puplick recalls that Wentworth brought forward land rights proposals to cabinet which were knocked back by cabinet.[35] He argued this in relation to the Wave Hill walk-off, which was a strike called by the Gurindji people of the Northern Territory in response to exploitation by a British company, Vestey Brothers. In April 1968, he visited Wattie Creek on the Wave Hill Station where the Gurindji people of northern Australia, southwest of Katherine, were camped. In a media release, he said:

> The Gurindji told me of their desire to hold and develop a small area of some eight square miles as their own home area and of their plans for improving it. With them I inspected the area which they wanted . . . In consequence I am now, as a matter of urgency, examining with all the interested parties the implications and the methods of resuming this area from the Wave Hill Lease, and making it available for the purpose for which it has been requested. This would, of course, require the payment of equitable compensation to the present lessees.

These proposals were ultimately superseded by the land rights announcements of the Whitlam and Fraser governments. However, Wentworth made one of the most farsighted but depressing statements in parliament in a Second Reading speech on state grants for Aboriginal programmes in 1969:

> I believe profoundly that the future of Aboriginal policy can be no better than the future of consultation with the Aboriginal citizens themselves. I am seeking to bring this about in a fuller fashion by two means. One is to assist wherever possible with seminar-type discussions, in particular those in which Aboriginals themselves take part. We have already given considerable help in this respect, and we have found the information and comment provided by such occasions very valuable. The other and more important is to push on with direct consultation with representative groups of Aboriginals by my Office and the Council for Aboriginal Affairs. The Government believes it is essential to provide Aboriginal

citizens with regular opportunities to make their desires and views
known to those at the centre of policy formation and as far as
practicable to help in the formulation of policy.

This captures the whole point of this historical chapter.
Wentworth, conservative member of the Liberal Party decades
ago, wanted to put the Indigenous voices at the centre of
policymaking. So it isn't a trendy 'Woke' thing. Regrettably, the
idea that Indigenous people would have a say over laws and policies
which affect them has not been the dominant theme within liberal
Indigenous policy. But it has been there on a consistent basis since
Wentworth's statement more than fifty years ago.

Holt's achievement has largely been forgotten in the great list of
achievements of Australian liberalism. I suspect this has happened
largely due to the limited text that exists on Liberals which is
a structural problem of too few books being published about
liberalism and liberal achievement. The Liberal Party is the party
of the free market and this has its own list of achievements such as
tax reform, labour law reform, trade agreements, and the like. The
people within the party choose to prioritise certain achievements;
to focus on them. Indigenous affairs has not been a vote-driver,
which is perhaps why Holt and Wentworth's achievements seem
marginal.

But it is also driven by limited marketing available to Holt and
his acolytes. This is due to both his time and his circumstances. A
prime minister delivering a constitutional reform today would have
a vast array of marketing resources both during and after the event.
Tom Frame says Holt is the only leader of a liberal democracy
to go missing in centuries, accordingly, his bizarre death hurt his
legacy. He didn't get to write an autobiography explaining what

he regarded as his key achievements, undertake a round of media interviews, and be available. Prime ministers with similar tenures in the twenty-first century have been able to nominate their key achievements in their books and media appearances. Both prime ministers Kevin Rudd (2007-2010 and 2013) and Malcolm Turnbull (2015-2018) have made the case for what they regard as their legacy achievements: the National Apology to the Stolen Generations and the delivery of marriage equality. These opportunities were not available to Holt and the almighty squabble between the Coalition parties as to who would replace Holt meant there was little time for reflection on Holt's tenure.

Fraser government

The Fraser years delivered significant progress in Indigenous affairs. Fraser's biographer, Philip Ayres, argues that the Fraser period represented a break with past practices in Indigenous affairs: "it was consultative and far less paternalistic." Most importantly, Malcolm Fraser delivered land rights. Fraser's later biography says, "during Fraser's time, Aboriginal policy was more or less bipartisan, the differences between Whitlam and Fraser were matters of detail and implementation."[36] Yet at least one Aboriginal contemporary judges Fraser to have been the better of the two. Charles Perkins said in 1998:

> I found out that on Aboriginal affairs he was absolutely A1. He was tops. He was the best of them all on Aboriginal affairs. And Gough is good but you know the problem with Gough . . . sometimes he thinks he started everything and you know, he didn't. Fraser was very good on Aboriginal affairs and he produced the goods.[37]

This is consistent with the account given by Fraser's sometime Minister for Aboriginal Affairs, Fred Chaney:

Fraser was committed to Aboriginal Australia. The party went to the 1975 election with an Aboriginal affairs policy which was sustained over the life of the government. This ensured policy consistency across the three ministers over the life of the government. Fraser cared, was involved, and stood behind his ministers.[38]

Land rights loom large in any assessment of the Fraser years, as does extensive discussion of treaty and makarrata. As ever, land rights and treaties are intertwined. And of all the words uttered in Indigenous affairs over the centuries, perhaps the following words are the most moving and least known:

For the first time in history an Aboriginal is introducing a Government measure into the Parliament . . . it places in the hands of Aboriginal people important instruments for their own advancement.

These are the words of Senator Neville Bonner speaking on the Aboriginal Development Commission Bill in 1979. Bonner was a Senator in Malcolm Fraser's government. Fraser himself was a man who appeared to have genuine interest in Aboriginal affairs. Eggleton suggests that it was Fraser who carried on the Holt legacy within the Liberal Party. Sinclair's conclusion concurs : "[Fraser] followed the Holt line."[39] Puplick is certain Fraser was more than Holt's natural heir, however, because Fraser took a broader view of Australia's place in the world as an advocate for human rights. Puplick says:

Malcolm was absolutely committed to stopping all forms of racial discrimination. Holt thought it was [about being] just and fair. Fraser saw it was essential to have a clean house if we were going to advocate on South Africa. We couldn't say aboriginal people of South Africa were entitled to land if we weren't going to do the same.[40]

Fraser and Margaret Simons say in their biography of Fraser that although the problems in the policy space were immense, "Fraser and his ministers held firm to the view that there could be no solution that did not respect the right to self-determination. Aboriginals, like all other Australians, should be free."

Fraser was a keen fisherman, which provides certain insights. John Mangos was in the press gallery in the early 1980s when Fraser was prime minister. Mangos recounts a tale of the prime minister stopping his plane in Anchorage, Alaska, to personally attend to a fishing tackle shop during a long-haul trip. A prime minister stopping an air force jet to visit a fishing shop is unthinkable today, but it shows how much Fraser enjoyed fishing. Fishing was something Fraser did when he visited the Northern Territory. Former journalist and political advisor Brian Johns, an official with the Department of Prime Minister and Cabinet travelled with Fraser to the Todd River in the Northern Territory:

> He was wearing some kind of worsted suit, and he sat down, this great tall man, in the dust and asked this Aboriginal man what he wanted from government, and the man told a long story about wanting a bore so they could get water, and how they had asked for it and it was never done.

Interactions of this nature were new—prime ministers started regularly visiting remote communities during the 1970s—both Whitlam and Fraser travelled throughout Northern Australia. Another fishing adventure with land rights activist and 1978 Australian of the Year, Galarrwuy Yunupingu, which became a talking point for decades, is discussed below. Fishing became a metaphor for comfort: too much comfort and insufficient listening: politicians came to fish, not to listen. These barramundi featured in Galarrwuy Yunupingu's powerful 2008 *Tradition, Truth and Tomorrow* and Noel Pearson's brilliant 2014 essay, *A Rightful Place.* As a keen fisherman myself, I regret the negative reflection upon fishing, but it illustrates the poor job the political class have done of listening to Indigenous people.

Fraser's era saw the latest iteration of Indigenous representation in the form of the National Aboriginal Conference in 1977. Between 1975 and 1983, the Fraser government sought input from the National Aboriginal Council—which later became the Aboriginal and Torres Strait Islander Commission—on the major issues of the day, as Fraser came to terms with land rights, calls for a Makarrata, and seemingly the first serious attempts to deal with the ongoing cost of ingrained welfare cultures. Self-determination was often referred to as 'self-management' during the Fraser years. Part of the agenda was the creation of the Aboriginal Development Commission with Charles Perkins as its inaugural director. Perkins described it as the "high point in Aboriginal affairs in an economic sense."[41] If the focal point of Holt's tenure was the referendum, Fraser's was land rights. Meanwhile, makarrata deliberation did not conclude during Fraser's term despite it being his policy.

Land rights

The signature achievement of the Fraser era was land rights. In 1976, the Fraser government introduced the *Aboriginal Land Rights (Northern Territory) Bill*. This was the policy of the Liberal Party at the 1975 election, but had also been the policy of the defeated Labor government led by Gough Whitlam. Whitlam's government had established the Woodward Royal Commission in 1973, which had recommended a system of land rights. Land rights legislation in the Northern Territory was the culmination of decades of work that included the Yirrkala Bark Petitions presented in 1963. The legislation provided a scheme where lands could be granted to traditional owners, generally through trusts or land councils. By

2018, almost half of the Northern Territory had been granted back to traditional owners. Similar laws were subsequently passed in New South Wales and South Australia.

In order for these recommendations to become Liberal Party policy, Fraser had to secure support for them within the Coalition party room. Peter Baume, a backbencher at the time, but subsequently Minister for Aboriginal Affairs (1980-82), recalls:

> I led the charge in the party room by suggesting that we actually go further. The National Party were against it and were goggle-eyed. They didn't know what to say. It was a preemptive strike—we got in before they had time to organize. Chaney and Bonner worked with me. They said, "Don't listen to him [Baume], and the present bill is fine. That's how we got it through."[42]

Ian Viner, Minister for Aboriginal Affairs from 1975 to 1978, maintains that great credit is also due to the Country Party—later the National Party—leader, Doug Anthony, because there had been great antipathy to land rights from the Country Party as well as throughout the pastoral and mining sectors. Viner was the minister responsible for negotiating the laws. This was done against the strong opposition of the Northern Territory's Country Liberal Party government.[43] Viner notes there were very tough internal debates in the party room. After the party room came the parliamentary committee stage. In this case, the bill went to Philip Ruddock's committee.

Ruddock recalls that the Committee stage of the bill's review was a foregone conclusion after the party room stage because of Labor's support. But he saw other motivations. He saw Fraser as a leader wanting to avoid risk:

> Fraser wanted to generate across the board support for his government after the Dismissal [of the Whitlam government]. Fraser wanted to minimise the risk of civil disobedience. His lack

of preparedness to pursue industrial relations reform is testament to the fact.[44]

Viner was strong. He addressed the critics, explaining, "Unfortunately, the suggestion of land rights to some arouses intense opposition and even charges of Apartheid. Still other detractors of our land rights policy are in the state of shock that a Liberal Government would be so radical—as if social reform were an exclusive prerogative of the left."[45] Viner recalls that after the passage through the party room, "I called in Bill Stanner [of the Great Australian Silence fame] to help me with my Second Reading speech; to demonstrate their ancient connection to land. I made the point that this was the first time that customary law was recognised in Australian law. The Land Rights Act was a remarkable achievement both legally and politically."[46]

Viner told the House of Representatives on 4 June 1976:

> Aboriginals associate identifiable groups of people with particular 'countries' or tracts of territory in such a way that the link was publicly reputed to express both spiritual and physical connection between living people and the dreamtime . . .

Viner's 1976 speech in the House could be delivered in 2021 with very few changes. This is a rare feat. Next the bill had to get through the Senate. Viner credits Bonner and Chaney for helping in the red chamber. He held the vote on the final bill back until he inserted an amendment which allowed new land councils to be created. This was not one of Woodward's recommendations, it enabled the Tiwi Land Council, for example, to be established promptly.[47] With the federal parliament enacting land rights, Fraser's government encouraged the States to do the same. They were successful in South Australia but not in Viner and Chaney's home State of Western Australia. Baume says of the two leaders:

> Malcolm Fraser was excellent. As Minister for Aboriginal Affairs, I found he never ever let me down. The fact is he ended up with the right kind of decisions. Doug Anthony [National Party Leader and Deputy Prime Minister] was very good to deal with on land rights matters when I was the minister.[48]

The consistent view on Fraser and land rights is that his was an extraordinary achievement. Fred Chaney, Minister for Aboriginal Affairs from 1978-1980, recalls:

> Land rights was an extraordinary step for the Liberals and was also embraced by its Coalition partner. I am proud of the Liberal Party's record on Aboriginal affairs at that time. Getting all party federal support for land rights was an incredible achievement. I remember saying to Malcolm, "You know there's no votes in this," but we both agreed it was the right thing to do.[49]

This accords with the Fraser administration's public position at the time: Viner told the National Press Club in July 1977 that "the major achievement has been the Land Rights Act, proclaimed in January this year. This Act provides for Aboriginals to gain title to existing reserves and traditional land in the Northern Territory. But its wider significance, in my opinion, is the recognition this law gives to the special cultural identity of the Aboriginal people within the life and laws of Australian society."[50] In 2020, Viner maintained that "Fraser was 100% in favour. It was our policy. He was very supportive. When the Queensland premier, Joh Bjelke-Petersen, said he 'wouldn't sit down with Aboriginals for dinner,' Fraser said he was having lunch with them today."[51]

Fraser admitted he had few allies on this front; he noted Bonner, Chaney and Ruddock amongst his supporters.[52] Viner says, "I encouraged [the South Australian premier] David Tonkin to pass similar laws in South Australia to cover the Anangu Pitjantjatjara

Yankunytjatjara lands. To his great credit he did. They mirrored the laws we passed for the Northern Territory."[53] Land rights was a big step forward which Fraser did because he knew it to be morally right despite the political opposition he faced.

Treaty and makarrata

The Fraser government adopted the policy of makarrata in 1980. In Fraser's words, it means "the end of the dispute and resumption of normal relations."[54] Alan Missen, a Liberal Senator for Victoria, was known as the great supporter of makarrata. But it never made much of an impact on the party room.[55] Missen was the original chair of a lengthy parliamentary inquiry into makarrata. The word *makarrata* comes from the Yolngu language, in which it means coming together after a struggle.[56]

The historical record shows Fraser's government and his minister, Fred Chaney, speaking openly about the concept in play. They didn't like the idea of a *treaty* as it implies the existence of an external nation with which Australia could treat. There are two ideas here. The first is the idea of a *treaty*, which is a broad agreement between two national groups. The second is *makarrata*, which is a concept developed through the National Aboriginal Conference for domestic purposes. In March 1981, Chaney addressed the government's policy in response to the National Aboriginal Conference's request to pursue a makarrata:

> The Government is prepared to acknowledge prior Aboriginal occupation of Australia. However, in pursuing the development of the Makarrata concept the Government wished it to be clear that any agreement . . . must reflect the special place of Aboriginal and Torres Strait Island people within Australian society as part of one Australian nation . . . the Government . . . cannot legitimately

negotiate anything which might be regarded as a 'treaty', implying as it does an internationally recognised agreement between two nations.

The government, therefore, sought to pursue a makarrata during the Fraser administration. Fraser was operating in an environment where the National Aboriginal Committee had developed clear requests of the Commonwealth which were as follows:

- land rights over former reserves and national parks and recognition of traditional rights to hunt, fish, and gather on Crown lands;

- a national Aboriginal bank, tax exemptions, and payment of 5% of Australia's gross national product for 195 years as reparations;

- one seat per State in the House of Representatives and the Senate to be reserved for an Aboriginal or Torres Strait Islander person;

- self-government of Aboriginal communities and respect for Aboriginal customary law;

- return of artefacts and artworks and control over research on Aboriginal people; and

- dedicated Aboriginal schools, medical centres, and legal aid.[57]

In response, Chaney sets out the Fraser government's response:

- return of tribal lands including sacred sites and freehold title—should be taken up by the National Aboriginal Committee with the States separately [in other words, utilise the land rights schemes where they exist because the States have the lands, and where we control lands, we have legislated land rights (in the Northern Territory)];

- compensation in cash as percentage of gross national product or percentage equivalent to Aboriginal proportion of total Australian population—Government cannot agree to such a fixed percentage nor to any fixed financial commitment into the future [in other words, no separate scheme in addition to land rights];

- reserved seats for Aboriginal people in Commonwealth Parliament — Government cannot agree for such reasons as doubt about "necessary public support" and questioning of the merits of such systems in other countries; special representation in State parliaments and local government bodies is a matter for the States [in other words, no, because it will be heavily opposed and it hasn't worked offshore]; and

- compulsory employment of a fixed proportion of Aboriginal people in government bodies—Government will continue to promote existing schemes designed to stimulate employment and promotion opportunities for Aboriginal people in the Commonwealth sphere, but does not believe a system whereby Aboriginal employment is subject to a rigidly fixed formula is appropriate[58] [in other words, we will employ more people but we will not establish quotas].

The Fraser government remained open-minded about a makarrata, as long as it wasn't a treaty—which it believed carried international connotations and would be inappropriate.

Chaney said of makarrata: "In the Fraser years, he indicated we would be prepared to negotiate a treaty. The idea of a treaty shouldn't be offensive to Liberals as collective Aboriginal identities are now an accepted part of Australian law and in a treaty negotiation both sides have to agree." Makarrata remained a fluid concept. It remains fluid today. But it was sent to an inquiry. A Senate Committee was established in 1981. Its report was entitled, *Two hundred years later: Report on the feasibility of a compact or Makarrata between the Commonwealth and Aboriginal people.*

The Senate commissioned the inquiry during the Fraser government and undertook the bulk of its work during the Fraser years, but reported to the Hawke government towards the end of 1983. Labor Senator Michael Tate chaired the backend of the inquiry with Liberal Senator Robert Hill in the deputy chair position (he would later become Leader of the Government in the

Senate). In 200 pages of evidence collected over two years, its primary recommendation was:

> The Government should, in consultation with the Aboriginal people, give consideration as to the preferred method of legal implementation of a compact, to the insertion within the Constitution of a provision along the lines of section 105A, which would confer a broad power on the Commonwealth to enter into a compact with representatives of the Aboriginal people. Such a provision would contain a non-exclusive list of those matters which would form an important part of the terms of the compact, expressing in broad language the types of subjects to be dealt with.

In other words, the Constitution should provide a framework for internal treaties. This was the position put at the beginning of the Hawke government. Given the report did not emerge during the Fraser administration, it is difficult to assess the level of attachment to the concept of makarrata. The work of the committee was not enacted by the Hawke government and was superseded in time. The 'enabling' Section 105B seems not to have been pursued further, in part because it had become outdated. The recognition of native title rights in the 1992 *Mabo* case meant that land rights, one of the main components of a treaty in the past, was resolved by the courts and the parliament. Ultimately, the issues concerning Fraser and the Committee's inquiry have to some extent been 'enabled' by other means in the years following the review. The Committee was at best unclear about the need for new constitutional provisions in any event.

Conclusion

Viner in 1977 was still channeling Wentworth from a decade earlier when he said, "I would hope to encourage the growth of this confidence by direct involvement of the Aboriginal people in decision making processes . . ." In his later years, Fraser remained interested in the issues without necessarily changing direction as he had done on other issues. But on Aboriginal issues, he was consistently supportive of their agenda throughout his life. Fraser became disenchanted with the Liberal Party as the party went through internal philosophical ructions in the 1980s and 1990s after his government's defeat in 1983. Fraser's involvement with the Liberal Party waned after a failed bid for the Federal Presidency of the Liberal Party in 1993. Towards the very end of his life, Fraser let his membership lapse.

This is not uncommon. In the liberal tradition, there is a reasonably healthy amount of free thinking. John Gorton ran against the Liberal Party as an independent and Menzies himself is believed to have voted for the Democratic Labor Party. One of Fraser's final policy contributions was to argue for a voice-like structure in the Vincent Lingiari Lecture in 2000:

> Let us move to self-government. This does not relate to setting up a separate state. It doesn't relate to establishing a separate sovereignty, to the division of this country. Aboriginal leaders have spoken overwhelmingly of their wish to contribute to Australia. They have not spoken of separation. Self-government can apply to running your school, running local community health centres and services, or perhaps a cultural association, matters which might in some cases be undertaken by local government. The Canadian experience is a positive one, it is not a frightening one. We should learn from other people, especially where their experience is so relevant to ours.[59]

This advocacy for more self-determination or control is a pitch for a mechanism like that anticipated by the Uluru Statement.

When it came to Indigenous affairs, Fraser had to deal with two major issues: land rights and makarrata. The Senate committee into makarrata ran for more than two years. This meant that the policy of makarrata which Fraser adopted at the midpoint of his tenure did not get properly canvassed during his administration. The makarrata committee reported to the Hawke government, which did not act on its recommendations. A makarrata was embodied in the last act of the next prime minister, Bob Hawke. He said, "my final act as Prime Minister, on the morning of 20 December 1991 in Parliament House, was to receive for permanent display the Barunga Statement . . ." Yunupingu said of Hawke's tears, "I am sure that his tears are for his own failure—we have no treaty; his promise was hollow and he has not delivered." As a result, in the twenty-first century makarrata remains an unclear concept beyond land rights and financial compensation which have now been delivered in many parts of Australia. Putting it to a committee was probably the right move.

The fact is, Fraser made significant progress early in his term as prime minister. His government delivered the land rights which today help support a real achievement wherein almost half of the Northern Territory belongs to Indigenous Australians. There is no doubt about the credit. The credit goes to Fraser and the small group of Liberal MPs who pushed land rights legislation through with Labor's support. In large part, a treaty is actually about land, which can be delivered through land rights. The financial component was later aided by the actions of State governments, which made financial settlements. On the issues Fraser did not agree, such as reserved parliamentary seats, his government said so. His place as a deliverer on national reconciliation is assured because of land rights. This is consistent with Perkins's verdict on Fraser.

Howard government

Journalist and historian Paul Kelly described Indigenous policy during the Howard years as "the missed opportunity of Australian conservatism . . . As reconciliation evolved in its symbolic and practical dimensions, it became a natural position for a conservative leader. Labor was in denial of this truth and the Liberals were blind to their opportunity."[60]

Howard was and remains a greatly admired figure because of his leadership on the economy and security in particular. He was a liberal reformer who delivered the big changes that Fraser could not—such as a consumption tax. Howard clearly marked out a serious economic policy legacy, the best Liberal economic reformer. Major reforms which had alluded Australia, such as a consumption tax and liberalisation of workplace laws were achieved. From a political perspective, winning a goods and services tax and a tax-mix switch was the hardest reform of all of the deregulation era (1983-2000), because—as with tariff reform—it involved the risk of a scare campaign. But Howard took risks to do the right thing. This led to signature achievements which sometimes hurt his own core constituency—most notably the gun control laws of 1997.

On Indigenous affairs, Howard faced a hard task coming after Paul Keating, who had made it one of the primary focuses of his time as prime minister (1991-1996). Like Howard, Keating was forced to respond to events occured early in his term that drove his focus on Indigenous affairs. Keating's approach to Indigenous affairs was part of his brand differentiation from Hawke, who ended his term having failed to deliver the treaty that the Barunga Statement called for, and which he had promised to deliver. Keating then made a mark where Hawke did not. Just six months after

Keating took the job from Hawke, in June 1992, the *Mabo* decision extinguished the notion of *terra nullius*—a legal milestone like no other in Australian history. Keating put a framework around Mabo with the 1993 Redfern Park Speech and the *Native Title Act 1993*. Keating became an activist as prime minister on Indigenous affairs.

By the time of the 1996 election, both major parties were aware that Keating's plans on Aboriginal issues were a vote loser. Journalist and author Pamela Williams wrote in her summary of the 1996 campaign:

> The pollsters' report also showed that voters felt Keating was not concentrating on issues of importance such as jobs, the economy and the future for young people. They saw Keating's big picture issues such as the flag, the republic and Mabo as irrelevant. The blue-collar voters were particularly hostile to the proposed Mabo legislation.[61]

Keating was no unifier, and it is very hard to imagine him chaperoning a successful constitutional amendment such as constitutional recognition, which requires the Australian population to provide approval.

In terms of Indigenous affairs, the Howard years, unlike the Holt and Fraser era, did not have a signature achievement in Indigenous affairs. This is despite Howard changing tack at the last minute on constitutional recognition. This does not mean the events were insignificant or that time and effort was not expended. Howard spoke good words on reconciliation, and Reconciliation Place in Canberra was established in his time.

Delivering a significant change like constitutional recognition would have required Howard to become an activist. His instinct was to be a unifier, he had styled himself very differently from Paul Keating. Howard wanted Australians to be "relaxed and comfortable" about their history. Howard did not put a proposal on the table on constitutional recognition until the past few months of his tenure. His Sydney Institute speech on reconciliation with only six weeks of his eleven-year term remaining was amongst his best. Parts of this speech remain a formula for success at a future referendum. Howard was a risk taker. He risked his political capital to get a better tax system and to advance labour law reform, but he did not take a risk on Indigenous affairs; perhaps because the proposal for a constitutional amendment was not fully developed during his tenure.

Noel Pearson described "a sense of loss" at Howard's end in Paul Kelly's book, *The March of Patriots*: "We haven't completed the circle—bringing the responsibilities and rights agendas together properly." What Pearson describes was Howard's failure to use the immense political capital coming from the side of politics which had delivered substantive change in the past. This is understandable as Howard did not seek to persuade the Australian people, whom he won over in four consecutive general elections, that there ought to be such a significant change as constitutional recognition. Six major issues in Howard's tenure included the history wars, the continued fallout from Keating's native title legislation, the issue of an apology, ATSIC, the tone and form of reconciliation, and the intervention on the Northern Territory.

Apologies

The question of whether to offer an apology on behalf of the nation loomed large over Howard's time. It was persistent, and perhaps even dominated discussion of social policy during

Howard's tenure. It concluded with the National Apology to the Stolen Generations by Howard's successor, Kevin Rudd. The idea of an apology emerged from the *Bringing Them Home* report in April 1997 which set out the forced separation of children from their families, to be known as the Stolen Generations. The report recommended reparations, a public education campaign and official apologies from all Australian parliaments. Howard would not say sorry for the policies of forced removal of children which the report said was "genocidal". He didn't like the idea of what he called a "retrospective apology" but said, "I was sorry that our Indigenous citizens were treated poorly in so many respects. But the idea that the current generation can apologise for the deeds of the past generations, I had a problem with that." Howard genuinely did not believe a retrospective apology was appropriate. Other Liberals disagreed. State Liberal leaders Jeff Kennett of Victoria and Kate Carnell of the Australian Capital Territory offered clear apologies in response to the report.

Within months of becoming prime minister, he had to speak at a convention, at which the audience expressed their annoyance. They turned their back on Howard. He hadn't been in office very long, so this wasn't a response to his track record as PM, it could only have been a response to his election promises at most. At the convention Howard said that he didn't want to dwell on the past:

> It will not work if it is premised solely on a sense of national guilt and shame. Rather, we should acknowledge past injustices and focus our energies on addressing the root causes of current and future disadvantage among our Indigenous people.

Peter Shergold, his departmental head, told Paul Kelly, "I think it severely shook his confidence in dealing with Aboriginal leaders. He was always wondering what sort of reception he might get. As a professional politician Howard knew how to behave but with Aboriginal leaders he was often apprehensive, you saw it in the body language."[62]

With the benefit of hindsight, we can see the sense in which the Aboriginal political class believed Howard had been disrespectful of the Aboriginal experience of dispossession and discrimination. But by turning their backs on him, they showed disrespect to his office. It was a bad start. Shergold's perspective suggests that the ramifications of this went beyond Howard's approach to the apology. They impacted his whole approach to Indigenous affairs and dealing with Indigenous people.

Paul Kelly said there was no philosophical reason for Howard's opposition to an apology: "There was nothing in Liberal Party ethos that dictated its rejection of an apology . . . Like Saint Peter, Howard had three opportunities to apologise—in 1997, 1999, and 2000—and he refused on each occasion."[63] There were Liberals who were keen on an apology at this time. Indeed, the former Minister for Aboriginal Affairs, Peter Baume, gave a speech to the University of Tasmania on 17 October 1997 in which he said:

> So may I now, as a former minister for Aboriginal Affairs, on behalf of all such of my generation as may wish to join me, that in respect of the Stolen Generations we are sorry for what was done, sorry for the hurt, sorry for the tragedies we caused, sorry for the unhappiness we inflicted, sorry for the lives we ruined, sorry for the families we parted.

There would be no apology and symbolic gestures were not high on the list of priorities. The Sydney Harbour Bridge walk, a symbolic offering of reconciliation, occurred in May 2000 to coincide with the centenary of Federation. There was much publicity at the time about Howard's preference not to engage

with the bridge walk. Howard's Deputy, Peter Costello, told Paul
Kelly that Howard raised it in cabinet to avoid a number of senior
ministers walking. Costello said of Howard's bridge intervention:

> He said I hear some of you might be walking and this won't look
> good, so we had better have a collective decision . . . I just said if we
> have to have solidarity why not show solidarity by walking. I said
> this would be a very powerful statement, a real story . . . When you
> think about it: who can be against reconciliation? Even to this day,
> I can't understand why you wouldn't walk. My view is we grossly
> mishandled this.

Philip Ruddock told me he was authorised by Howard to walk
across the bridge as the relevant minister, but Tony Abbott and Joe
Hockey also walked, which raises the question as to why there was
so much consternation over the bridge walk. The remarkable thing
seems to be that Abbott and Hockey were prepared to defy Howard
on this. It says something about how strongly Abbott felt, that he
was prepared to defy Howard on this matter.

History wars

The history wars took off during Howard's tenure. He appeared
concerned that attempts at rebalancing away from the Great
Australian Silence cast an aspersion upon majority Australian
culture and achievement. Stanner's framework, the Great
Australian Silence, kicked off the history wars in the late 1960s
by explaining that Australians prefer not to think about the plight
of Indigenous people. Later historians, like Manning Clark, then
adopted a position that Australians must think about it and must
act differently. By the 1990s, historians on both sides of the debate
were drawn in and the debate became known as the history wars;
Stuart McIntyre with Clark supporting the critique of Australian

history, and Geoffrey Blainey defending Australia. In hindsight, it appears to be a fairly unsophisticated debate because it forced people to take a side. This over-simplification of our history did little to drive a positive debate in pursuit of national reconciliation.

The history wars were a big deal during Howard's tenure. There was even a book called the *History Wars* which was written by historian and author Stuart McIntyre and Anna Clark who is the granddaughter of the historian Manning Clark. By the late 1990s, the school curriculum required a more balanced presentation of perspectives such as the historical texts of historian Henry Reynolds and the contemporaneous words of people like academic Robert Manne being contrasted to Geoffrey Blainey.

Howard's position in the history wars was made crystal clear just eight months into his eleven-year premiership, where he referred to Geoffrey Blainey's "black armband" view of Australian history in the 1996 Menzies lecture:

> There is, of course, a related and broader challenge involved. And that is to ensure that our history as a nation is not written definitively by those who take the view that Australians should apologise for most of it. This 'black arm band' view of our past reflects a belief that most Australian history since 1788 has been little more than a disgraceful story of imperialism, exploitation, racism, sexism and other forms of discrimination. I take a very different view. I believe that the balance sheet of our history is one of heroic achievement and that we have achieved much more as a nation of which we can be proud than of which we should be ashamed.

With this statement, he adopted Geoffrey Blainey's 'balance sheet' approach to assessing Australia's history. Blainey argues that, on balance, the positive well and truly outweighs the negative. Howard took a side. He was not stuck in the middle. Blainey's Sir John Latham Lecture was the vehicle for introducing the 'balance sheet' approach to Australian history. He contrasted the 'three cheers' view of Australian history with the alternative 'black armband' perspective. Blainey worried that Australia will "deprive [young Australians] of their inheritance if we claim they have little to be proud of." He thinks the black armband supporters like historian and author Manning Clark have swung the pendulum too far and are damaging the broader "on balance" achievements of the nation. He blames Clark for twisting Bob Hawke's government for changing the official slogan of the bicentenary from "the Australian Achievement" to "Living Together".

But Blainey accepted the utility of the black armband position. He says, "The black armband view of history might well represent the swing of the pendulum from a position that had been too favourable, too self-congratulatory, to an opposite extreme that is even more unreal and decidedly jaundiced."[64] While Blainey's is a generally fair and reasonable reading of the history, it feels like Howard boxed himself in on these issues at the beginning of his premiership as he didn't want to promote the black armband position. He wanted to bury the black armband view of history. He liked Geoffrey Blainey. He liked *Quadrant* magazine. He didn't like the black armband view of Australian history. He did like the 'three cheers' view of our history. It probably made matters worse that the Victorian academic Robert Manne, who was a major critic of Howard's economic and social policy agenda, was working the black armband brigade. Because he had taken such a strong position on the history wars, there wasn't a great deal of room for Howard to work on the agenda.

The historian and academic Ann Curthoys argues that Howard sought to do two things to "minimise, but not do away with entirely, recognition of past injustices towards Aboriginal people . . . [and] a return to the politics of assimilation and reject more recent ideals of self-determination, autonomy, and the need for a treaty."[65] The fact that Howard regularly spoke of the error of past policies and placed recognition in the Constitution on the table shows this isn't a balanced assessment—the truth is that Howard's focus was elsewhere. Keating made Indigenous affairs central to his premiership. He did not make significant achievements in the policy space, but neither did Bob Hawke. Howard was strong on economic policy. He was a great economic reformer and remains the benchmark for assessing such reformers. Equally, after Keating, many Indigenous leaders were suspicious of Howard and it showed in their public interface with the prime minister in his early years in the role. Howard did try to engage with the issues—he didn't ignore them but he didn't approach them in the way Curthoys believes he should have.

Reconciliation

The third issue went to the question of formal recognition in Australia's Constitution. In the year leading up to the 2007 federal election, Noel Pearson started engaging with Howard about constitutional reform, suggesting that he should channel Holt's successful 90% referendum as, he wrote, "I don't believe Labor could unite conservative and progressive Australia on this issue."[66] The proposal Howard set out for recognition reflected his view that a nation doesn't make a treaty with itself and his position as a constitutional conservative.

He rightly said at the end of his time in office that "this nation spent (and wasted) a lot of time in the last thirty years toying with the idea of a treaty implying that in some way we are dealing with two separate nations. To me this goal was always fundamentally flawed and something I could not support."[67] Instead, Howard put forward a proposal based on the following idea:

> We must find room in our national life to formally recognise the special status of Aboriginal [people] and Torres Strait Islanders as the first peoples of our nation. We must recognise the distinctiveness of Indigenous identity and culture and the right of Indigenous people to preserve that heritage.

This was the start of the long national debate on recognition in the Constitution which has continued for a decade and a half. The full promise that started this debate was as follows:

> I announce that, if re-elected, I will put to the Australian people within eighteen months a referendum to formally recognise Indigenous Australians in our Constitution—their history as the first inhabitants of our country, their unique heritage of culture and languages, and their special (though not separate) place within a reconciled, indivisible nation.

In calling this his "new settlement", Howard committed the Liberal Party to a referendum on a constitutional amendment for which he sought to invoke Holt's success by securing "the sort of overwhelming vote achieved forty years ago at the 1967 referendum." Although the influence of Pearson is clear, Howard's words were genuine: he didn't pretend to be someone he was not.

Although Howard spent so much political capital avoiding an apology, he established a debate on constitutional recognition. Howard's formulation of constitutional recognition would survive his government and live for another ten years until the Uluru Statement in 2017. Yet it was not to be. The Howard government was defeated by Labor and the new prime minister, Kevin Rudd, had a different set of priorities.

Native Title

In December 1996, the *Wik* decision was made by the High Court against Queensland. This followed the *Mabo* case of 1992, which held that native title existed under Australian common law and that the notion of *terra nullius* was erroneous. *Mabo* established native title. It also established that native title was extinguished if the Crown granted freehold over the land to someone else.

What the decision in *Mabo* left uncertain was what happened to native title if the Crown granted a pastoral lease. This was a special form of land title. It didn't give the pastoralist ownership of the land in the sense that freehold title does, but it had been thought to be as good as freehold for all intents and purposes until *Mabo* came along. Now, as a point of law, if freehold had been granted, native title would have been extinguished. The Court made that clear. If it remained Crown land, then native title could continue unless it was extinguished in some other way. The uncertainty was whether a pastoral lease extinguished native title in the way that a grant of freehold title extinguished it. The Court was forced to consider this question in *Wik*. It held that a pastoral lease did not necessarily extinguish native title in the way that freehold did.

It was known that this issue had not been resolved by the High Court in *Mabo*, and so it would have to be addressed either through legislation or by a subsequent High Court decision to resolve the common law on this point. Coming just four years later, *Wik* held that native title is not necessarily extinguished by the grant of a pastoral lease and that native title can coexist with non-Indigenous interests in land. SBS summarised the decision thus:

> The High Court determined that pastoralists did not have exclusive

rights to the land. The Wik and Thayorre people were then granted the right to Native Title in two areas of land. While the decision wasn't exactly momentous, the decision itself simply stating that the existence of a lease did not extinguish Native Title, for the Wik people and for all First Nations people this was a closer step to formal recognition and self-determination as original and initial owners of a land that had been colonised.

As a result of the court decision, Howard developed a ten-point plan to balance the competing priorities of the Indigenous groups, the pastoralists, and the miners. In May 1997, Howard addressed the anxieties in the community which had been whipped up about the *Wik* decision:

> I also need in the name of truth and in the name of a frank discussion of this issue to repudiate the claim that my ten-point plan involves a massive hand-out of freehold title at taxpayer expense. That is an absolute myth, it is absolutely contrary to the fact and I absolutely repudiate it. I believe that the plan which I have put forward provides an equitable balance between respect for the principles of Native Title, as laid down in the *Mabo* decision, and the very legitimate interests of pastoralists and others in securing certainty in carrying on and planning their activities.

Later, Howard said upon the release of his cabinet papers that "the *Wik* decision left us confused. When the High Court said . . . they could coexist, that created a problem and I don't think I handled the next six months all that well. I wanted to get everybody together but it went on too long. It looked like the government was drifting." Given that there was so little goodwill towards Howard on the Indigenous leadership, how could he deal effectively with them? They had disrespected him; he had missed the opportunity to apologise. Howard was hardly in a position to command the confidence of all concerned, even if he wanted to do so. But by early 1998, parliament passed the 293 amendments to the *Native Title Act*. In doing so it entrenched the position of native title in the Australian legal system forever. The Liberal Party had accepted the legitimacy of native title. Land rights had already been a feature of the federal system since 1976, but native title was another plank towards rebalancing the country.

Aboriginal and Torres Strait Islander Commission

The Aboriginal and Torres Strait Islander Commission was established in 1990 by the Hawke government, as the primary governance structure for Indigenous communities. It proved to be a constant source of conflict for the Howard administration. The Howard government's solution was to abolish ATSIC, declaring that the experiment of Indigenous representation was both a failure and over. It was abolished in 2005 after there were ongoing governance problems—including allegations of corruption at ATSIC. There were mixed views about taking the step to remove ATSIC altogether as it removed the consultation mechanism. The minister of the day, Amanda Vanstone, said in 2018, "In hindsight, [abolition] might have been a mistake."

In his letter to Howard one month before the latter's defeat, Pearson lamented the removal of ATSIC and distilled the point that needed to be made:

> Indigenous governance institutions are important—however it is their interface with Australian governments that is the nub of the question. The point of ATSIC was to establish an interface with governments, rather it established an Indigenous affairs ghetto away from the main game.[68]

The only interface with governments following the abolition of

ATSIC has been advisory committees set up by prime ministers—there has been nothing as formal in its structure as ATSIC. There is no doubt that the void created by ATSIC in 2005 helped form Pearson's view in 2014 that there should be a mechanism for consultation, such as a Voice.

Northern Territory intervention

In 2007, John Howard introduced a set of policies in response to the *Little Children are Sacred* report. The report was commissioned by the Northern Territory government which claimed neglect and sexual abuse of children in Indigenous communities had reached crisis levels. Declaring the Indigenous child abuse to constitute a 'national emergency', Howard said that drastic action was required in isolated Northern Territory townships because "in the end, the duty of care to the young of this country is paramount." Under the plan, Aboriginals in seventy-three targeted remote communities faced bans on alcohol and pornography, and their welfare payments became conditional on school attendance and child health. Such was the urgency, the military was called in to help roll out the Northern Territory Emergency Response—known as the Intervention—under Howard's Indigenous Affairs Minister, Mal Brough. To say it was controversial would be an understatement.

Restrictions were imposed and individual agency was reduced under the Intervention. In terms of national politics, Howard faced little opposition to the Intervention. The government was able to take advantage of its Senate majority to push through the legislation. Labor leader Kevin Rudd saw no electoral advantage in criticising the Intervention, framed as it was in terms of deviance, dysfunction, and abuse of vulnerable children.

The National Indigenous Council and Reconciliation Australia backed the crackdown, but some Indigenous leaders condemned what they described as heavy-handed tactics and a lack of consultation. Howard probably best described his strong-arm tactics when he said, "We are dealing with children of the tenderest age who have been exposed to the most terrible abuse from the time of their birth and any semblance of maintaining innocence of childhood is a myth in so many of these communities." The Intervention occurred at the very end of Howard's long premiership and it occurred when, for the first time since 1967, there was no formal Aboriginal representative body. Abolishing ATSIC without creating a replacement left the government without any mechanism for formally consulting Indigenous people in relation to the Intervention. Whatever the merits of the Intervention, it occurred without the type of consultation that would be expected—then and now.

Summary

Howard left office with ATSIC abolished, no apology, and no signature achievement in Indigenous affairs. Yet there had been the consolidation of the native title regime by the Howard government which entrenched it into Australia law and policy. There was also the creation of Reconciliation Place in Canberra. The history wars ran throughout Howard's decade in power. The history wars seem to have pushed the nation apart without yielding any positive developments. Did the prime minister really need to take such a strong position? It feels like his decision to commit himself wholeheartedly to this battle left the prime minister with minimal, if any, middle ground in which to pursue reconciliation.

The Indigenous people were never going to accept their treatment in the first two hundred years of modern Australia as the "blemish" that it was for Howard:

> In facing the realities of the past, we must not join those who would portray Australia's history since 1788 as little more than a disgraceful record of imperialism. Such an approach will be repudiated by the overwhelming majority of Australians who are proud of what this country has achieved although inevitably acknowledging the blemishes in its past history.

The Howard position ended with Howard. It did not stretch into the next government. Rudd said sorry in February 2008. The apology appears on the walls of virtually every school. The vast bulk of the Liberals supported the apology. The Liberal Party elected Brendan Nelson as its leader, and the new leader of the opposition said:

> We formally offer an apology to those Aboriginal people forcibly removed from their families through the first seven decades of the twentieth century. In doing so, we reach from within ourselves to our past, those whose lives connect us to it and in deep understanding of its importance to our future. We will be at our best today—and every day—if we pause to place ourselves in the shoes of others, imbued with the imaginative capacity to see this issue through their eyes with decency and respect.

Nelson's strong speech marked another period of great interest in Indigenous affairs. Nelson wisely embraced the legacy of Neville Bonner, too often forgotten by the liberal movement. Asked to nominate his main achievement, Bonner said, "It is that I was there. They no longer spoke of boongs or blacks. They spoke instead of Aboriginal people."

Abbott government

The Liberal Party returned to power for the first time since 2007 in September 2013 under Tony Abbott's leadership. While Abbott was philosophically aligned with Howard, he was the next generation and was personally committed to pursuing the form of recognition that Howard put on the table before leaving office. Abbott came in after Labor's chaotic period of government, when they changed leadership multiple times between 2007 and 2013. The cycle was repeated under the Coalition. One major issue dealt with by the first Rudd government was the apology to the Stolen Generations.

In *Battlelines*, Abbott wrote that "the Rudd Government's apology was a 'feel good' gesture."[69] Abbott's instincts were to unite. He described Australia, using Pearson's formula, as having "an Indigenous heritage, a British foundation, and a multicultural character because it was true and also because it gave just about everyone something to be proud of."[70] Abbott picked up where Howard left off—in his speech to the 2013 Garma Festival in Arnhem Land his position on constitutional recognition was:

> As far as I'm concerned, speaking now as a conservative, the great unfinished business of the constitutional process was back in the 1890s. The great gap in what was done then was that it didn't involve a single Aboriginal person and yes that failure was a failure of those times . . . As far as I am concerned Indigenous recognition would not be changing our Constitution but completing our Constitution; and until this is done our country will not be whole.[71]

His commitment to deal with the constitutional reform was almost identical to Howard's 2007 promise—only a shorter timetable would apply:

> But within twelve months we will publish a proposal for

constitutional recognition and we will establish a bipartisan process to try and bring that about as soon as possible. This should be a great unifying moment for our country; a unifying moment perhaps to surpass the 1967 referendum or the national apology.

Abbott was rightly proud of the fact that he was the first Liberal prime minister to have spent a lot of time in remote Indigenous communities:

When I was a new Member of Parliament I travelled regularly to Alice Springs and to some of the communities around Alice Springs such as Hermannsburg, in particular I would try to take the time and learn from the experience from the insights of Charlie Perkins, one of Australia's great Indigenous leaders of an earlier generation. And then once I became a minister I tried to ensure that every year I spent at least a week actually in some of the more significant Indigenous communities in which I had substantial responsibility.

Abbott would inherit the report from the Expert Panel on Constitutional Recognition of Indigenous Australians. The expert panel, which was co-chaired by anti-racism advocate Mark Leibler and Patrick Dodson, had been commissioned by the Gillard government to advise on options for how Indigenous peoples could be recognised in the Australian Constitution. Its report had been tabled in parliament in 2012. Its core recommendations were to acknowledge the contribution and presence of Indigenous Australians and insert a prohibition on racial non-discrimination. The new section on recognition would be as follows:

Section 51A Recognition of Aboriginal and Torres Strait Islander peoples

1. Recognising that the continent and its islands now known as Australia were first occupied by Aboriginal and Torres Strait Islander peoples;

2. Acknowledging the continuing relationship of Aboriginal and Torres Strait Islander peoples with their traditional lands and waters;

3. Respecting the continuing cultures, languages and heritage of Aboriginal and Torres Strait Islander peoples;

4. Acknowledging the need to secure the advancement of Aboriginal and Torres Strait Islander peoples.

There would be separate amendments on racial non-discrimination and another on language. Politics got in the way of the expert panel's report. Rudd failed to deal with the report Gillard commissioned before he lost government. Abbott's approach was to set up a parliamentary committee. This was chaired by the first Aboriginal member of the House of Representatives, Ken Wyatt. Wyatt's committee recommended three versions of the above statement of recognition be debated by both the Senate and the House of Representatives before putting the question to the people. Wyatt's inquiry also recommended that section 25 of the Constitution, which deals with voting and races, be repealed along with some tweaks to the races power in section 51 which was amended in 1967. This report was tabled in parliament in June 2015. By September, Abbott was gone. Abbott was clearly a supporter of recognition—but it remains unclear how he would have handled a Voice.

Turnbull government

Malcolm Turnbull was the first Australian prime minister to speak in an Aboriginal language in federal parliament. This reflected his "respect to the culture and the people on the land on which we were deliberating. But perhaps more importantly, it spoke to resilience and renewal."[72] Turnbull described his approach to Indigenous affairs in two ways. First, he attributed his commitment to "stopping doing things to Indigenous people and start doing things with them" to the South Australian educationalist, Chris Sarra—a Goreng Goreng man of the Gladstone region in Queensland.

Secondly, he generally described himself as an optimist, who would rather spend time talking about Indigenous success—especially through business and procurement—rather than talking about failures all the time—the kind of issues people in remote outback communities tended to be concerned with. His view was that "the vast majority of Indigenous Australians live in cities, like the rest of us, and are getting on with their lives, raising families, working, learning and investing."[73]

On constitutional issues, Turnbull was the prime minister who received the Uluru Statement. He explains his position on constitutional recognition as it existed before the Uluru Statement as follows: "I was very interested in it. In fact, it was an issue at the time of the republican referendum back in '99. And we collaborated and supported a change to the preamble to acknowledge Aboriginal people and the entirety of our human history. But sadly, that was defeated at the same time as the republican referendum."[74]

Turnbull acted on Abbott's plan to establish a Referendum Council. The council was jointly appointed by Turnbull as prime minister and Bill Shorten as opposition leader in December 2015. The council's job was "to advise the Prime Minister and the Leader of the Opposition on progress and next steps towards a successful referendum to recognise Aboriginal and Torres Strait Islander peoples in the Constitution." It looked at the reports of both the Expert Panel on Constitutional Recognition of Indigenous Australians and the Joint Select Committee on Constitutional Recognition of Aboriginal and Torres Strait Islander Peoples. In May 2017, it met with Turnbull and Shorten in the cabinet room.[75]

The Voice emerges

The Referendum Council finished its work in June 2017, when it adopted the Uluru Statement with a Voice to Parliament as its central recommendation for a constitutional amendment in its final report. Before receiving the final report, Turnbull observed that the Uluru Statement consisted of big ideas but was short on detail. After receiving the report, Turnbull said that the Referendum Council was tasked with drafting an amendment and instead offered a column of smoke. Its report recommended that the Government should implement the Uluru Statement's call for a Voice, but the Referendum Council did not do the hard work to draft an amendment to this effect, as it had been tasked with doing. Turnbull was right to call out the Referendum Council for failing to meet its mandate— but it was not necessary to handle it this way. The report was considered by cabinet, which reached a unanimous decision not to accept the Referendum Council's recommendations. Accordingly, the Voice was rejected by the Turnbull Government. The cabinet decision was leaked in the *Courier Mail*. The prime minister then had to issue a press release clarifying the government's position.

After the almost immediate rejection of the Referendum Council's recommendations, Turnbull's government laid the foundation for the revival of the Voice. In March 2018, a Joint Select Committee would be agreed between Turnbull and Shorten to investigate the Voice. The Committee, chaired by Labor Senator Patrick Dodson and Liberal MP Julian Leeser, was to be truly influential but would not report until the Morrison government emerged from the dramatic leadership challenges of August 2018. Turnbull said of their appointment: "They are both very capable people . . . I don't doubt they did a good job."[76] The Turnbull period marked the end of the line for symbolic recognition which had started with Howard in 2007. It had eaten up ten years. It was the start of the Voice to Parliament concept, which while not supported by Turnbull, his actions set in train its revival under the leadership of Scott Morrison. The Voice to Parliament concept is canvassed in detail in the next chapter.

Ten years of stalemate

Having observed both Tony Abbott and Malcolm Turnbull up close, it is true that the men had little in common with each other. They differed in style and approach. So it isn't surprising that whereas Abbott would spend a week in a remote community, Turnbull would visit Indigenous businesses. But they were both cold on the signature proposal of their day—the Voice. Abbott said of the Voice that recognition should "come in a way that brings all of us together and this proposal, for a further level of Indigenous representation, was unlikely to achieve that." Both Abbott and Turnbull governed through the period of political assassinations, as did Rudd and Gillard. Both major parties changed their leadership rules to stop the practice of the revolving door of prime ministers. The real policy cost of the period of assassinations has been well documented. In the Indigenous affairs space, it meant that proposals, committees, and processes slowed or had to be reset.

Valuable time was lost over the decade. Frustrating as the whole thing was, Australia wasn't ready to go to a referendum in 2017. It has taken time to understand that recognition is about recognising the need for Indigenous voices to be heard; for a bottom-up rather than a top-down mechanism for hearing these voices; and, to understand what the mechanisms would look like, before trying to amend the Constitution to make provision for Indigenous people to be recognised.

It was a heady period. Unlike the Fraser and Howard eras, was a succession of leaders during this period of government. Turnbull overthrew Abbott. The enmity between the two was real as Abbott stayed on in parliament and differentiated himself on policy from his successor on energy policy and same-sex marriage. But Turnbull has publicly rejected any suggestion that Abbott differed on the Voice. Like the Howard era, progress was slow. There is nothing on the scale of the 1967 referendum or land rights.

As set out above, the very limited understanding of the contribution Australian liberalism has made to Indigenous affairs is bad for Australia. We have seen above that there is a record of achievement which is material. Of course, not everything has been rosy under the Liberal Party. But people in the Liberal Party at the national level have taken risks to deliver big and contested reforms like land rights. This is in addition to all the 'firsts' at the national level, such as the first Indigenous parliamentarian (Bonner) and first minister (Wyatt), as well as the quiet achievements of the Menzies era, like voting rights. Furthermore, we have forgotten Harold Holt, who delivered the federal power in the most successful referendum in our history. We only remember him for his demise and perhaps dismantling the white Australia policy. A limited understanding of the past can limit our ambition in the present. Labor does much better in the mythology department. Labor has done good things as well, Whitlam was solid on land rights and Keating put native title on a statutory footing. Ken Wyatt has described Keating's Redfern Speech as "a moment of truth telling in our nation's history." By his own admission, Hawke didn't deliver. The image of Whitlam pouring red dirt into the hands of Vincent Lingiari, of the Gurindji people in the Victoria River region of the Northern Territory, is iconic but it doesn't tell the full story. Ultimately, delivery is more important than imagery and we in the Liberal Party have a record to build upon.

The past lives in us

Australia's past is not a different country. It is the same Australia and Australia's history weighs heavily on Indigenous people—it should be better understood across the community. As Charles Perkins said, "We cannot live in the past; the past lives in us." What Perkins is getting at is the fact that it is the negative aspects of the past that live in us as much as the positive aspects. Thus, we need to confront the living legacy of racism. The public may see this emerge solely around Australia Day, when there are various proposals to remove statues of James Cook or Arthur Philip. A discussion around statues can be most unsophisticated. It shouldn't be.

The notion of the Great Australian Silence was first coined six decades ago. Stanner said:

> It is a structural matter, a view from a window which has been carefully placed to exclude a whole quadrant of the landscape. What may well have begun as a simple forgetting of other possible

views turned under habit and over time into something like a cult
of forgetfulness practised on a national scale.

In other words, we venerated Federation, the newly named
continent, and the Anzac legend for most of the twentieth century
without considering the Indigenous perspective.

Stanner said, "It is incontestable that few of the great affairs
of the past took any sort of account of the continued Aboriginal
presence."[77] For example, new statues to mark the 250th
anniversary of the Endeavour's arrival have been erected at
Kurnell in Southern Sydney. However, this started to change in
the wake of Stanner's work and the efforts of people like Manning
Clark and Henry Reynolds to rebalance Australia's history. In
recent years, there has been progress. When I was educated at the
beginning of the century, both perspectives were taught as part of
the history syllabus. Historian Anna Clark says:

> The murmurings have since turned into a groundswell: Indigenous
> histories have become increasingly prominent and Indigenous
> perspectives are now mandated across school curricula.
> Conspicuous public and political debates over Australian history
> are further indication of how this counter narrative has become a
> significant historical lens.[78]

I am not one for the culture wars or the history wars. Too many
of the proponents of either case are blinded by ideology or are
pushing barrows for other reasons. I have never wanted to judge
people outside of their historical contexts. I have never thought
pulling down statues was going to improve people's lives or the
nation. It is a denial of history when we should be honest about
our history. There are mixed views on this question. Good people
can disagree. Being honest is the most important part of being at
peace with our shared history. Australia has a history which has

been both good and bad. This doesn't mean it is one or the other. It means it is both. As set out above, Blainey attacked Manning Clark's efforts to rebalance our history as a black-armband reading of our history. This led to a decade-long debate between the black-armband and the three-cheers perspectives.

Both perspectives are valid and can be taken together. In his thought-provoking essay on the history wars, Damien Freeman identifies peace as the aim of a successful society and distinguishes between an "ordered peace" and a "just peace". He suggests whereas Blainey shows Australia has succeeded in achieving an ordered peace, the treatment of the Indigenous population shows a failure to achieve a just peace. So Freeman concludes that "Australian history involves both success and failure, we are justified in feeling positively about it." Unlike Blainey, he does not present it as a balance sheet. It is not that, on balance, the success of an ordered peace outweighs the failure of a just peace. He invites us to conclude that we are justified in feeling positively about our history on account of the success of achieving an ordered peace and peace is always desirable. What we can now see is that Freeman shows that Blainey has identified the achievement of an ordered peace as something to feel positively about and the failure of a just peace as something to feel negatively about. When we then consider how we should feel about Australia as a peaceful society, Blainey is right that we should feel positively about our history—but not, Freeman thinks, on balance.[79]

Australia has been very successful but we can never balance away the past injustice because it lives in all of us. Perhaps it is dormant in most of us—but it is not dormant in the hearts and minds of Indigenous people. It comes through in the brilliant writing of Noel Pearson, Stan Grant, and Melbourne University anthropologist Marcia Langton of the Yiman people in the upper Dawson River region of eastern central and southern Queensland.

On a global basis, Australia's success as a country is not in doubt. Australia performed amongst the very best nations during the Covid-19 global recession on both health and economic fronts. The same can be said for our comparative performance in prior pandemics like the 1918-1920 Spanish flu and our response to the 2008-09 global financial crisis. And while the country rebounded and strongly grew after the Second World War, the Indigenous people, including men who had served in uniform, were excluded. That's why I keep coming back to this point that for many Indigenous Australians, Australia has not been a good country. This makes them the outliers.

That is the truth and the narrative was oversimplified during the history wars era. I believe politicians can be too defensive about this matter. People make mistakes; nations get things wrong. When I have been wrong, I have said so. I am a proud, patriotic Australian and I can honestly state my view that our history has been both good and bad. Ensuring that we are honest with ourselves about our history is important.

Freeman says Blainey identifies the treatment of Indigenous people as a failure to achieve a just peace. They both agree that we should feel negatively about this failure. Freeman points out that Blainey has this much in common with Manning Clark and the black-armband historians: all agree that we should feel negatively about the failure. Does this mean we should feel 'shame' or 'regret', which Freeman reminds us are very different?

It is difficult to say. I feel immense regret about past practices. Some days I feel dreadful about the lack of goodwill that I sometimes find exists towards Indigenous people. However, I did not personally undertake the dreadful policies so I do not feel that I should personally feel ashamed.

The conversation about 'shame' and 'regret' is a serious one, and it affects the way we deal with the present issues. I respect the fact that many people do feel shame, some feel regret, and others feel both. What Freeman points out is that as both shame and regret are negative feelings, the fact that we all feel negative feelings—albeit different negative feelings—might be a sufficient foundation for the national project of our moving forward together. It is enough that all Australians agree that they feel negatively about the failure to achieve a just peace, even if the specific negative feelings that people feel differ from one another. We should not try to force people to feel a particular emotion, or condemn people who feel different negative emotions when confronting the failure to achieve a just peace. As Stan Grant told me, "It doesn't mean people need to feel shame personally."

These feelings should implore us to spend more time thinking about our lot as Australians and how our country came to be. We clearly need to do so. Carlton footballer Eddie Betts captures this need when he says, "All we want is for the rest of Australia to understand us and to acknowledge what has happened to us." While the education syllabus has been rebalanced, there are many elements of Australian culture and life which do not sufficiently include the nation's rich Indigenous culture. In New Zealand, the Haka is performed by white Kiwis. There is more we can do to promote the wonderful unique culture and art of Indigenous

Australia. The Great Australian Silence has been rebalanced in our history books—but it is yet to rebalance our national life.

Section 51, Clause XXVI:
    Means that laws with respect to Aborigines are the responsibility of the States, apart from those living in the Northern Territory.

    The effect of this clause is that there is little uniformity in the laws governing Aborigines in the States and Territory.

RIGHTS ENJOYED BY ABORIGINES ON SETTLEMENTS & RESERVES IN 5 STATES & THE NORTHERN TERRITORY

	N.S.W	VIC.	S.A.	W.A.	N T	QLD.
Voting Rights (State)	Yes	Yes	Yes	No	Yes	No
Marry Freely - - -	Yes	Yes	Yes	No	No	No
Control Own Children	Yes	Yes	No	No	No	No
Move Freely - - -	Yes	No	No	No	No	No
Own Property Freely -	Yes	No	Yes	No	No	No
Receive Award Wages	Yes	No	No	No	No	No
Alcohol Allowed - -	No	No	No	No	No	No

Extract from the Federal Council for the Advancement of Aborigines and Torres Strait Islanders' *Petition for a referendum to remove discrimination against Aborigines from the federal constitution* (1963).

Image courtesy of the University of Queensland Library.

Reference code: FVF622.

First Australian campaigners meet with Prime Minister Harold Holt seeking support for the 1967 referendum.

From left to right: Gordon Bryant, Faith Bandler, Harold Holt, Doug Nicholls, Burnum Burnum, Winnie Branson, and Bill Wentworth (February 1967).

Image courtesy of the National Archives of Australia.

NAA: A1200, L62232.

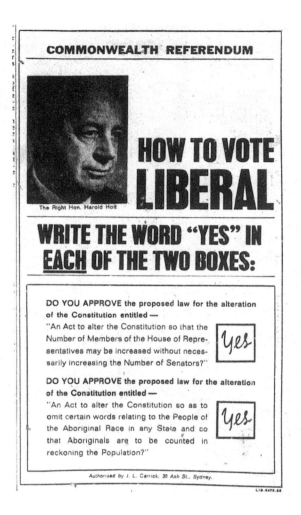

How-to-vote print advertisement appearing in the *Sydney Morning Herald* on 27 May 1967, prepared by the New South Wales Division of the Liberal Party for the 1967 referendum.

The Prime Minister, Malcolm Fraser, with Chair of the Northern Land Council, Galarrwuy Yunupingu, and Minister for Aboriginal Affairs, Ian Viner, holding up fish caught on a trip during his official visit to the Northern Territory in 1978.

From left to right: unidentified, Galarrwuy Yunupingu, Malcolm Fraser, and Ian Viner.

Image courtesy of the University of Melbourne Archives.

Reference code: 2005.0104.00159.

Copyright holder: Department of Foreign Affairs and Trade.

Bill Wentworth standing at the junction of station tracks on the Wentworths' trip through Katherine, Pine Creek area, and Arnhem Land, 1966.

Image courtesy of Australian Institute of Aboriginal and Torres Strait Islander Studies. Reference: WENTWORTH.B06. CS-000170321.

Sam (left) and Bill Wentworth (right) on top of a rock outcrop at the Ruined City, also on the Wentworths' trip through Katherine, Pine Creek area, and Arnhem Land, 1966.

Image courtesy of Australian Institute of Aboriginal and Torres Strait Islander Studies. Reference: WENTWORTH.B06.CS-000170229.

Senator Neville Bonner at his desk in 1976.

Image courtesy of the National Archives of Australia.

NAA: A6180, 18/12/79/7.

Uluru Statement from the Heart (2017).

Maruku Artists, Uluru Statement from the Heart ©Rene Kulitja, Christine Brumby, Charmaine Kulitja, Happy Reid/Copyright Agency, 2021.

Ken Wyatt is sworn in as Minister for Indigenous Australians by Australia's Governor-General, Sir Peter Cosgrove, at Government House, Canberra, on 29 May 2019.

Photo: Tracey Nearmy/Getty Images.

Sean Gordon, Senator Andrew Bragg, Richie Ahmat and Rachel Perkins at Parliament House in Canberra on Wednesday 24 July 2019 for Senator Bragg's first speech in the Senate.

Photo: Alex Ellinghausen.

2

Nhaway Today—listening to Indigenous people

THE LESSON FROM HISTORY is plain and clear. The nation's policies have not established an Australia which delivers for everyone. In large part, this is because there has been too much paternalistic policy, insufficient consideration of the perspectives of Indigenous people, and a political failure to meet commitments to Indigenous people. The Great Australian Silence has permeated policymaking process as Australia's political history shows. Australia will require new approaches and new institutions if we are to deliver a national reconciliation.

Current state

This chapter moves from the past into the present. In doing so, it moves into the listening mode. It does two things: it presents the current state of affairs and sets out the key policies sought by Indigenous advocates. In this way, it engages with the critical Indigenous material such as the Uluru Statement, land rights laws, and symbolic matters such as the Aboriginal flag and the Australian National Anthem.

The present is built on the past. The past is not a different country in Indigenous Australia. The past looms large for many Indigenous families. It is intergenerational. When you listen, you find that the Uluru Statement offers one pathway that Indigenous people offer for Australia to address the legitimate concerns which have arisen from the Great Australian Silence. Black Lives Matter offers another pathway. These are the broad policy options which are on the table.

This chapter sticks to the principal issues of reconciliation as set out by Indigenous advocates. It does not set out the detailed answers on Closing the Gap, which is a formula to ensure there is parity of social and economic opportunity in Australia. The Closing the Gap framework was developed following the National Apology to the Stolen Generations in 2008 and was substantially revised under the Morrison government in 2020. A national reconciliation without economic parity is neither credible nor sustainable, which is why the Closing the Gap framework is of the utmost importance. In so many ways, the economic participation which will be driven by the Closing the Gap framework of Indigenous Australia and national reconciliation go hand in hand. But the focus of this book is considering and evaluating the policy options on the table for national reconciliation.

I take on this task as a person who is not Aboriginal or Torres Strait Islander. I am taking my own advice and listening and engaging. Engaging is good—but listening is key. I think too many people who are not Indigenous are worried about saying the wrong thing, so engagement falls away. It is possible to engage and have a say without being boxed in by divisive identity politics. Helen Pluckrose and James Lindsay wrote in their 2020 book, *Cynical Theories*, that postmodernism—which underpins identity politics—is designed to have a "chilling effect on the culture of free expression . . . as good people self-censor to avoid saying the wrong things."[1] This doesn't mean overturning the practice of *doing with* rather than *doing to*. All the Indigenous people I know recognise the value of non-Indigenous advocacy for national reconciliation. Rachel Perkins, a filmmaker from the Arrernte people of central Australia and the Kalkadoon of the Mount Isa region in Queensland, spoke in her 2019 Boyer Lectures about the relationship between present challenges and the past: "The past has made us. We are its inheritors, for better or worse, and this is now our time." In linking the past to the present and future, Perkins goes on to implore Australians to get behind the Uluru Statement. Responding to this Statement takes up the bulk of this chapter.

Where we stand today

In assessing the standing of Indigenous people in contemporary Australia, the first step is to determine what is most important to them. What are the day to day issues facing Indigenous Australians? Beyond the notion of governments listening to them and providing more community control, there are issues, indeed there are many problems. Marcia Langton tells me the most important issue is economic participation, which is determined by education. It is hard to disagree with this. Economic participation is the key to everything. Education is addressed by Closing the Gap. Only once this is done, can economic participation be achieved, and this is the most important factor. What this means is that education is a condition precedent for the most important factor (economic participation).

You cannot have a fair society without a strong economy. That has long been my basic ethos, but it is also true in the Indigenous sphere. Without an economic basis, a community will not function. The same is true for an individual: without skills or capacity to generate an income, there are very limited prospects. That is the key point Warren Mundine, a former Liberal candidate from the Bundjalung of the north coast of New South Wales, made in a Centre for Independent Studies report on economic development:

> The gap between Indigenous and non-Indigenous Australians exists for one reason: too many Indigenous people do not participate in the real economy. Lack of economic participation underpins all areas of Indigenous disadvantage. And lack of economic participation is the main barrier to achieving parity. Economic participation is about having the financial means to meet your needs, without government benefits or charity,—which means having a job or operating a business—and the foundations necessary to do that, the most important of which is education.[2]

Indigenous people of Australia are far from homogeneous. Priorities depend on perspective. The development of an Indigenous middle class means that there are very different perspectives of what's important inside broad and diverse Indigenous Australia. It is a mainly urbanised population living in suburbs like Penrith and

Blacktown, and large towns like Shepparton and Dubbo with 20% of the population living in far remote areas. In the far-flung regions, mining, tourism, and pastoral industries offer genuine employment and economic development prospects.

That's why the relationship between miners, for example, and traditional owners is so important—because mining is the only game in town in some parts of Australia. The economic value of Indigenous businesses serving the mining sector range between $200 million and $350 million and the native title payments are estimated to be $3 billion in 2013.[3] The disastrous actions of Rio Tinto, in destroying Juukan Gorge's sacred sites in 2020, undermined decades of effort on the part of the company to build rapport and win the confidence of traditional owners.

At Juukan Gorge, Rio Tinto destroyed the Puutu Kunti Kurrama and Pinikura peoples' cultural site dating back 46,000 years in the Pilbara region of Western Australia. It was a putrid, criminal chapter in Australian history. It was an event worthy of a royal commission. Instead, there was a parliamentary inquiry which recommended a suite of changes to State and federal laws. The report states:

> The Committee's visit out to the Juukan Gorge site to see the devastation firsthand was quite distressing. The grief of the Traditional Owners was almost overwhelming for everyone who witnessed it. They had lost more than a piece of heritage—they had lost part of themselves, a piece of their living culture which was infused with the still present spirits of their ancestors and pregnant with the future stories of their descendants.[4]

How could this happen in Australia in 2020? It is any wonder many Indigenous people have no confidence in our institutions? State and federal heritage protection laws must ensure these events are not repeated whilst preserving the capacity for mining activity to occur in consultation with the traditional owners.

Generally, good economic opportunities are only available to people with skills. As the 2014 Forrest Review into Indigenous economic issues explains, "Given the fact that there is no employment gap, or disparity, for first Australians who are educated at the same level as other Australians, the full force of our community leaders and governments must pack behind the achievement of parity in educational outcomes as a national priority." Indigenous businesses have found it difficult to find capital. Forrest said in his 2021 Boyer lecture that a recent survey of 300 Indigenous-owned businesses revealed just 3.5% borrowed money from a bank to get started. Most relied on small amounts of savings. As Forrest said, "So why this two-track reality for entrepreneurs? Well, there are many reasons: systemic racism, intergenerational disadvantage and economic exclusion to name a few." In recent years, the Commonwealth's Indigenous procurement policy has boosted capital stocks for Indigenous businesses but there is clearly a shortage of capital available for investment. Accordingly, it is paramount that our settings on key Indigenous policies like land rights and native title schemes are calibrated to drive economic development.

For individuals, Indigenous and non-Indigenous alike, education is the key driver of opportunity, which is why it features prominently in the Closing the Gap framework. For other Indigenous people, getting an education is not the first priority. It is more basic. In the 1940s, an American anthropologist, Abraham Maslow, set out his "hierarchy of needs" which helps explain these differences:

> Needs in the lower categories have to be satisfied before needs in the higher ones can act as motivators. Thus a violinist who is

starving cannot be motivated to play Mozart, and a shop worker without a lunch break is less productive in the afternoon than one who has had a break.[5]

In other words, if living from day to day dominates your existence, there isn't much scope for economic development. Jacinta Price, an Alice Springs Councillor and Warlpiri Tanami woman of the West Australian-Northern Territory border region, identifies family violence as a major issue:

> With 23% of partner homicide victims in Australia being Indigenous, it is not time to worry about superficial concerns such as 'changing the date'. Let's prioritise fact over politeness and action over symbolism. Too many lives depend on this.[6]

Family violence is a problem in Australia. But is it particularly acute in Indigenous communities. Langton says violence is twenty to thirty times higher in Indigenous than in non-Indigenous communities. Price puts this down to cultural traits; Langton says it is driven by idleness. A 2018 report from the Australian Institute of Health and Welfare shows that "Indigenous women were 32 times as likely and Indigenous men were 23 times as likely to be hospitalised due to family violence as non-Indigenous women and men, respectively."

Noel Pearson has rightly said for many years that Indigenous Australians are "the most incarcerated people on the planet Earth." On life expectancy, the Australian Bureau of Statistics says an Indigenous Australian woman can expect to live to seventy-four years of age, while an African American woman can live to seventy-seven years of age. African American men live one and a half years longer than Indigenous Australian men.[7] While the comparative statistics are poor, there has been substantial progress. Statistics do not always tell the full picture—they do not tell us about the emergence of the middle class which Indigenous studies expert, Tim Rowse, has written about extensively with Stan Grant. The success is real as Grant set out in his 2016 Narrm Oration:

> Between 1996 and 2006 the Indigenous community in Australia was transformed. Numbers of educated well-paid professionals exploded. In just a decade, they increased by nearly 75 per cent. That was more than double the increase in the non-Indigenous middle class. By 2006 more than 14,000 Aboriginal and Torres Strait Islanders between the ages of 20 and 64 were employed in professional occupations. That's 13 per cent of the total Indigenous workforce.

The emergence of the middle class is a big step forward. But it can mean living in two worlds in some cases. This unfortunate trade-off is a driver of consternation within these growing cohorts. Brooke Boney, Today Show presenter and a Gamilaraay woman of the central northern New South Wales region, explains:

> It's difficult because people have to abandon their culture and leave it behind. This is a tragedy but it has boosted job prospects. It has been a trade-off. We want a middle class that can keep their culture and succeed.[8]

Pat Turner, an Aboriginal activist and campaigner of the Guranji in the northern region of the Northern Territory and the Arrernte of central Australia, identifies the persisting challenges of Indigenous Australia, and says these challenges need to be addressed in three ways: Closing the Gap, implementing the Uluru Statement, and a suite of symbolic changes to consolidate Australia. These are considered in turn below.

The Morrison Era

Closing the Gap—a new approach

The first package was set out by Indigenous people in partnership with Australian governments through the remodelling of the National Agreement on Closing the Gap targets in July 2020. This was Scott Morrison's first genuine attempt as prime minister to enter into a genuine collaboration—*doing with* rather than *doing to*. Marcia Langton and campaigner, Tom Calma, of the Iwaidja at the top of the Northern Territory, recently explained, "In July [2020], in the midst of our deliberations, the new National Agreement on Closing the Gap gave us a shining example of genuine partnership between Australian governments and Aboriginal and Torres Strait Islander peak organizations."

The new approach will be judged in years to come. I hope more Australians take an interest. Fred Chaney says of this approach, "The PM has set Aboriginal affairs on a new course in Closing the Gap by committing governments to a partnership approach . . . His change away from *doing things to* to *doing with* is a hugely positive step." There are both specific targets and process improvements which have been sought through the revised Closing the Gap framework. In summary, the sixteen targets include three large groupings: getting the basics right, getting out of jail, and setting up the economic foundation and cultural success.

First, the basics group includes closing the gap in life expectancy by 2031, ensuring 95% of Indigenous children attend early childhood education, getting 96% of Indigenous children to attain year 12 education or equivalent. It extends to getting 67% of young people (15-24 years) into employment, education, or training.

Secondly, there are the issues on incarceration. There are also targets on reducing detention and out-of-home rates by 30 and 45% respectively for younger people. There is a target to get the rate of adult incarceration down to 15% (a 50% reduction) by 2031.

Thirdly, there is a strong desire for economic and cultural connection to land and language. For example, one target is to increase the use of Indigenous languages. The sixteen targets as set by the Coalition of the Peaks cover a large amount of territory. The Coalition of the Peaks is a national grouping of fifty representative Indigenous bodies which have been convened to work directly with governments. In my travels across New South Wales, housing, policing, and jobs are always the top issues raised by the community members who I meet in places like Walgett or Kempsey. As Langton says, it all comes back to economic capability, from "creating parity—which is driven by education."[9]

Flag—a vignette

One thing which is almost universal is the belief that Australian governments need to listen to Indigenous people. Listening and collaborating leads to better results. This is not a trite line. I have witnessed examples where the failure to listen has led to very poor outcomes. In the limited time I have had in public office, there are few worse examples of where the government has not listened than the Aboriginal flag. The legal status of the Aboriginal flag is a vignette that is emblematic of the nation's mismanagement of Indigenous affairs. The Aboriginal flag first appeared in 1971 in Adelaide. It emerged from the Aboriginal Progress Association which had commissioned Harold Thomas, an artist from the Luritja people of central Australia. Thomas created the flag which features the red, black, and yellow colours. It was a flag of protest, of belonging to Country.

In 1972, the flag appeared at the Aboriginal Tent Embassy in Canberra. The Aboriginal Tent Embassy was established on Australia Day 1972 by four men who were protesting against the failure of the McMahon government to provide land rights. Some argue the use of the flag at the tent embassy was the unofficial birth of the flag as a national symbol for Aboriginal people. Perhaps remarkably, the flag became almost universally adopted and/or recognised by Australia's diverse groupings of Indigenous people.

As I have travelled widely throughout the State I represent to listen to Aboriginal people, the view expressed about the flag is generally the same everywhere from Redfern to Coonamble. Even the most ardent supporters of independent Aboriginal nations will heavily back the Aboriginal flag. There is immense pride in the flag and a sense of bewilderment that the flag is not freely available for use by Aboriginal charities and organizations. It is true that the flag is not the number one issue raised by the community—but it is seen as important. In November 2020, I spent a night in Brewarrina and had fish and chips with five local men who had never been politically active. I asked them their view on the flag, and they all spoke of the pride they feel when they see the Aboriginal flag. Looking after this flag is important to our country and its people.

2020 Flag Inquiry

In 2020, the Senate investigated the question of use of the flag. The evidence is overwhelming that Aboriginal people are ceasing to use the flag because of the complex arrangements for obtaining permission, some of which were put in place from 1995 by the

Keating government. Dozens of community groups, charities, and Aboriginal corporations gave evidence that they would no longer use the flag because they were being issued invoices or cease and desist notices. The issue was brought to a head by the Australian Football League, which decided it would no longer pay for the use of the Aboriginal flag. On the advice of its Indigenous Advisory Committee, the AFL stopped using the Aboriginal flag in 2020. The AFL's Stephen Meade said, "Absent a change in present arrangements that apply to the use of the Aboriginal flag, the AFL is concerned that there will be ongoing decreased use of the Aboriginal flag. The AFL sadly acknowledges that it will not use the Aboriginal flag, other than in flag form, absent a change in arrangements."

Removing the flag from the AFL's annual Indigenous round created pressure for change which few other organizations could have generated. It effectively turned off the tap to the businesses which had been licensed to use the Aboriginal flag. The AFL highlighted the plight of Indigenous charities and community groups being sent invoices they couldn't afford to pay. The AFL could afford to pay, but it chose to take a stand in order to highlight the difficulty smaller Indigenous organizations were facing when they wanted to use the flag. Charities and Aboriginal health and communities services told the Flag Inquiry they had received bills when they had used the flag or sought to use it. Alongside the AFL was a group called Clothing the Gap, set up to campaign for free use of the flag. The Aboriginal representative of Clothing the Gap, Laura Thompson of the Gunditjmara in southwest Victoria said, "I love the flag so much, it's heartbreaking. This flag has united everybody, all over Australia, from all the Aboriginal nations. The flag represented a struggle and a resistance movement, and now it just feels like a struggle to use it." The flag remains free for individual use but the way the licences operated, the Aboriginal groups like charities and health organizations were effectively captured as commercial organizations. Given the high use of communal organizations amongst Aboriginal people, this is a major problem. It is wrong to ask Aboriginal people to pay to use a flag which was designed for the community when the Australian flag can be freely used by any Australian citizen.

How did this happen? The gazetting of the flag under the *Flags Act* was bungled. It is a classic case of the government failing to consult with Indigenous Australians before acting—exactly what the Uluru Statement seeks to avoid through the establishment of an Indigenous Voice. In this case, the creator of the flag, Harold Thomas, was informed as an afterthought. He refused to be involved with the official recognition of the flag. On 14 July 1995, the flag was proclaimed by the Governor-General. The National Indigenous Australians Agency told the inquiry, "It appears from the archived ATSIC material that substantive consultation with Mr Thomas on whether the Aboriginal flag should be proclaimed did not occur. Further, the proclamation proceeded despite his known objection to it."[10] Subsequently, Thomas was forced to head to the Federal Court to secure his copyright on a flag which now has official status. Thomas said of the process of proclamation:

> The court case proved that I was telling the truth, from 1971 and up until 1997 when there was the court action. The story about that is that members of ATSIC then, which was a recognised institution created by the government to get people to vote in a democratic way, for individuals to speak and act on our behalf to the federal government; it was they who had the idea that the Aboriginal flag should be recognised under the Flags Act, and from that, the federal government accepted that . . . I objected it vociferously. Who are

these people to allow the Aboriginal flag to be blessed under the Flags Act? When I said we don't need that. We've never asked that for any symbols we've created for thirty, forty thousand years or more.

Justice Shepherd awarded the copyright to Thomas and concluded:

The fact is, however, that Mr Thomas, along with other members of the Aboriginal community, bitterly resented the flag being proclaimed in this way. In their view, the proclamation represented a usurpation of something which properly belonged to the Aboriginal people and not to the Australian people generally.

It is a good thing that the Aboriginal flag, a national symbol, is enshrined in the Flags Act. Its official title is the Australian Aboriginal Flag. But it is bad that the flag's usage has been constrained and the 1995 gazetting process has been discredited. Credit should be given to the Keating government for taking the initiative of gazetting, even though the process was totally bungled. The government should have reached agreement with Thomas before it had the flag proclaimed. Today, virtually every town hall or shire chambers in this huge country flies the Aboriginal flag. I took particular notice of the flags in Walgett in 2020 where the flags fly together. This is a long way from the Walgett of 1965 as described by Charlie Perkins.

The Australian Government is now seeking to right this wrong without injuring Mr Thomas. It is very important that Mr Thomas's rights are respected. The 2020 Senate Inquiry set out a very useful framework to bring the issue to a conclusion. The outcome I wanted it to seek was simply that the Aboriginal flag would be as freely available to use as the Australian flag. That should be the standard we pursue for any flag which is proclaimed as a flag of national significance. At the time of writing, sensitive negotiations are underway between the Minister for Indigenous Australians and Harold Thomas. When the Senate inquiry into the Aboriginal flag commenced, Wyatt filed a public interest immunity claim to protect the negotiations which was accepted by the committee chair—the impressive Labor Senator Malarndirri McCarthy (of the Garrwa in the top end of the Northern Territory and the Yanyuwa from the southern region of the Gulf of Carpentaria). I was a member of this inquiry and I found the inquiry to be a positive process which shed light on many issues which were misunderstood and/or culturally sensitive. The committee made two recommendations. Recommendation 1 was that the Commonwealth should not compulsorily acquire the rights to the Aboriginal flag. I believe compulsory acquisition would be a bad idea and an ugly precedent. Mr Thomas is a Stolen Generations man and the government removing his property is simply unacceptable. As Marcia Langton explained to the inquiry:

> I do not believe that the compulsory acquisition of the licences and/ or copyright of the Aboriginal flag is appropriate. First of all, there are constitutional issues and, moreover, it is my very strong view that the cultural property and the intellectual property of Mr Harold Thomas should not be compulsorily taken away from him. I say this for a number of reasons. One is that he is an Aboriginal person, and doing so would create a very bad precedent in terms of breaching the Constitution and any appearance of an act based on racial discrimination. Two, he is a member of the Stolen Generations, and for the government to cause him harm a second time would be unconscionable. His ownership of the rights in the Aboriginal flag has been affirmed by the Federal Court. The only way forward is for him to voluntarily relinquish all of his rights to the Australian government . . .[11]

Recommendation 2 urged the Commonwealth to effectively purchase the rights to the flag from Mr Thomas by aiming "to achieve a model for the future use of the Aboriginal flag by members of the community that is independent from government." It reinforces the first recommendation and the position the Minister for Indigenous Australians is seeking to land, but it also offers a model to maintain the flag in the future by setting up a body which "bears responsibility for maintaining the integrity, dignity of the flag and making decisions about the flag's use." The flag issue is a saga of the first order. It all could have been avoided if the government had worked with Harold Thomas. It again raises the question of how the Commonwealth should engage with Indigenous Australians. If the Commonwealth's negotiations are successful and the rights are acquired, a body of Aboriginal people should advise on the protocol and governance of the flag. One option I favour is to provide the Indigenous Voice, as proposed in the Uluru Statement, with a mandate to perform this role. Any such proposal should be decided in concert with Mr Harold Thomas, respecting his moral and legal rights.

Of the three Australian non-military flags of national significance, the Aboriginal flag is the only one with an uncertain status. Both the Australian and Torres Strait Island flag can be widely used by individuals, community groups, charities, and corporations subject to official protocol. For example, it is not permissible to affix text to the Australian flag. Incidentally, both are the products of competitions conducted by the Australian Government and the Torres Strait Island Regional Council respectively.

Symbolism

Symbolism is very important—it speaks to our identity as a people and as a nation. It has always been my view that symbols are important and I see the desire in the Indigenous community for our symbols to represent everyone. Aboriginal heritage can belong to all of us, and at the same time belong to Aboriginal people in a peculiar way. For instance, although the Aboriginal flag should be proclaimed as a flag of national significance, arrangements should be made for an Aboriginal council to safeguard it. We see this also with national parks where traditional owners have a role in their management. It is possible to reconcile the national interest and the traditional owners' interest in these parks. There are two different sorts of interests at stake. They don't have to be competing interests.

But symbolism should not be mistaken for tangible, practical change. Symbolic changes will not make an immediate impact on the closing the gap targets, for example. But worthwhile symbolic changes which bolster the legitimacy of the Commonwealth amongst Indigenous people can be an important component of a national reconciliation. There is always extensive discussion about national symbols and sounds. This is healthy.

Advance Australia Fair

A proxy in the debate emerged in October 2020 when the National Rugby League gave in to activists and temporarily cancelled the national anthem at State of Origin matches. The anthem was quickly reinstated. The NRL did the right thing to stick with Advance Australia Fair. The nation should not give in to division by cancelling or ignoring the symbols of Australia. Instead, we should look to giving a fuller expression to our history and Indigenous culture in Australian public life. This is exactly what the Australian Rugby Union did in performing the anthem in both Eora and English during December 2020—a magnificent spectacle. On New

Year's Eve 2020, Scott Morrison decided to change the second line of the first verse of the anthem from "young and free" to "one and free". This reflected the truth about the nation's age and our desire to be united as one nation—whether measured in ancient or modern terms. This has been a good change for which Morrison has not been given enough credit. This was the first change in the national anthem since Bob Hawke's changes including removing references to "Australian sons" in 1984. It is a change which complements the efforts to build a national reconciliation embodied in the Uluru Statement. It is not a choice between two things.

At each public event I conduct as a Senator for New South Wales, I recite an acknowledgement of country before the national anthem is performed. I have found they are complementary. When I opened my Sydney electorate office in 2019, my friend, Treasurer Josh Frydenberg, did the honours alongside filmmaker and founder of Blackfella Films, Rachel Perkins, who provided an acknowledgement of country. We then had a wonderful rendition of Advance Australia Fair by Natasha Gesto, a student of the Sydney Conservatorium of Music. Ceremony is important. People who attended on 25 September 2019 still tell me how they were moved by the union of the acknowledgment and the anthem; adding to our national life rather than subtracting works. Indigenous leader Pat Turner says of the welcome to country, "The Indigenous practice of acknowledging your place, and the place you are on, is something that has existed for thousands of generations. It is a way of being heard."

Canberra embodies the silence

The national capital, Canberra, brings the Great Australian Silence to life. It is a beautiful city, designed at the beginning of the twentieth century, and now more than one hundred years old. It is established and mature. The Parliamentary Triangle is the formal precinct of Canberra which contains national institutions. It features Parliament House, the High Court of Australia, the National Library, and other institutions as it stretches across Lake Burley Griffin. Robert Menzies drove the development of Canberra. He wanted to "build up Canberra as a capital in the eyes and minds of the Australian people."[12] The development of Canberra is a great legacy of Menzies, who opened the lake in 1964 and named it after the city's architect. He also presided over the opening of the National Library in 1968 when John Gorton was prime minister.

Building after building has been added to the Triangle, which points towards the Australian War Memorial—the focal point when looking out from an elevated position within Parliament House. Then there is Reconciliation Place, which is an annex of a flat precinct on the edge of Lake Burley Griffin. Reconciliation Place was established in 2000. John Howard said at the time:

> We have also committed to construct a site within the Parliamentary Triangle to be known as Reconciliation Place to honour the importance of reconciliation in the nation's life and to recognise the shared journey between the different peoples of the Australian nation. It will also include a memorial and depiction of the removal of children from their families as part of the very difficult and traumatic experience of the Indigenous people of this community.[13]

Reconciliation Place exists but there is no significant building reflecting Indigenous Australians inside the triangle on the scale of the National Library or the High Court. Visitors to another purpose-built capital, Washington DC, will be familiar with the spectacular National Museum of African American History and Culture. There is a proposal to rectify the void by establishing a large, built monument to Indigenous culture in Australia known as the National Resting Place. A recent parliamentary inquiry recommended this be built inside the Triangle:

> The Committee recommends that the Australian Government relocate the Australian Institute for Aboriginal and Torres Strait Islander Studies (AIATSIS) from its current location on the Acton Peninsula to a new location in Canberra's Parliamentary Zone . . . this should include public exhibition facilities, and a national resting place for repatriated ancestral remains that cannot immediately return to Country. The institution should be developed under the leadership and in comprehensive consultation with Indigenous Australians.

This bipartisan recommendation would entrench a national resting place inside the Triangle which would provide a culturally sensitive conclusion for the remains of Indigenous people taken abroad. Like the Tomb of the Unknown Australian Soldier, it would be a sombre and sincere expression of our desire for reconciliation, humanity, and unity. We should build it during this decade. A substantial building within the Triangle which is genuinely Indigenous will enrich the national capital and Australia. This is not to say that Indigenous culture and heritage is non-existent within the national capital. Most offices in Parliament House feature Aboriginal art. There are smoking ceremonies at the Opening of Parliament and acknowledgments of country are a regular feature.

We could do more to embrace this extraordinary culture which is unique to our country. Laura Tingle observes in her 2020 Quarterly Essay that the New Zealand prime minister wears a Maori ceremonial cloak on occasions of great national moment.[14] Ken Wyatt, Linda Burney, and Greens Senator Lidia Thorpe (of the Gunnai in the Gippsland region and the Ganditjmara of southwest Victoria), have all worn traditional cloaks, but why haven't the leadership? Would this be cultural appropriation? Not if there is respect shown and approval provided by the traditional custodians. I think a fuller embrace of this country's ancient culture from the nation's elected leaders is appropriate and overdue.

On cultural appropriation, I am certain we have come a long way from the appalling treatment of the Aboriginal artists Albert Namatjira and David Malangi. Namatjira, one of Australia's most celebrated artists, died in 1959 and the copyright to his work was taken on by the government's public trustee which sold his work for a song; thereby ending royalties to his family. Malangi's work was depicted on Australia's first one-dollar bill in 1966. Indigenous intellectual property expert Terri Janke says of this, "the selection of this art for the note involved no consultation with the artist . . . the Reserve Bank had not consulted anyone, assuming the design was the work of an 'anonymous and probably long dead artist'. It was of course a copyright work. David Malangi was given $1,000, a fishing kit and a silver medallion."[15] This was theft by the Reserve Bank which its Governor, 'Nugget' Coombs was said later to regret. But as we have seen, this pattern was effectively repeated by the Keating government in proclaiming the Aboriginal flag in 1995.

The Australian Government needs to show this cycle is broken forever. Filling the void in the Parliamentary Triangle would be a tangible demonstration of our efforts. It should be unifying and permanent. Adding a monument to the ancient Indigenous cultures in the seat of national government is a credible solution for believers in the Australian project. It is in keeping with the truth that Australia has a history which is both good and bad. Demonising Australia is not a credible solution. "Abolish Australia!" is the cry of the wrecker; the impotent activist, and will never deliver anything tangible for anyone.

Flags inside the Parliament

NAIDOC week in 2020 provided the opportunity for a stunt about the Aboriginal flag's use in federal parliament. The Senate select inquiry into the Aboriginal flag had recently reported and recommended that the negotiations between Harold Thomas and the Minister for Indigenous Australians continue. These negotiations are continuing. A motion was taken to the chamber seeking to display the Aboriginal and Torres Strait Islander flags in the Senate chamber. The Senate chamber was designed to be flagless. The State flags were displayed in the provisional (Old) Parliament House but the practice was not adopted at Parliament House upon moving to Capital Hill.

In 1992, Senator Ron Boswell successfully moved a motion to have the Australian flag permanently displayed in the Senate Chamber. Boswell said on 8 October 1992:

> I have been told that the Australian flag has not been in the Senate for 92 years. The Senate chamber of the old Parliament House had the State flags proudly displayed on the front wall—or the back wall depending on how one looks at it. When we came to the new Parliament House the flags did not follow us because it was said that they would not fit in with the decor of the Parliament. I can certainly say that a flag displayed here would present no problems to the architecture of this chamber.

There are now two Australian flags which sit behind the President's chair. These flags sit oddly on flagpoles and are clearly not part of the original design of the beautiful chamber. The House of Representatives appears to have been designed for flags. There are flags hanging near the ceiling. The motion would have added the two proclaimed Indigenous flags into the chamber. The Coalition voted against this motion, but this fact does not tell the full story.

Like many motions, this was a stunt or a gimmick without the possibility of constructive debate. Indeed, the use of such motions denies Senators an opportunity to address the issue at hand. They are designed to wedge opponents.

On the substantive issue, I believe we should permanently display Indigenous flags inside Parliament House. I think it is important that we avoid the practice of NAIDOC 2020, when both Indigenous flags were outside the House of Representatives but not the Senate. The national parliament should be proud of both flags and prepared to fly and display them prominently around the precinct—just as was done in the forecourt during NAIDOC week. At my request, the Parliamentary Library investigated whether any Aboriginal flags were permanently displayed inside Parliament House. The response from the Department of Parliamentary Services was:

> During special times such as NAIDOC week the Aboriginal and Torres Strait Islander flag will be flown from the ceremonial flag poles outside Parliament House. There are no Aboriginal or Torres Strait Islander flags on display inside the building, however, both Linda Burney and Nova Peris chose to have depictions of the Aboriginal Flag displayed in their official portraits. These are on display in the foyer of the Main Committee Room on level 1. Linda Burney is wearing a ring while Nova Peris is wearing earrings, both of which show the Aboriginal Flag.[16]

Accordingly, I wrote to the President of the Senate in November 2020 suggesting that both the Aboriginal and Torres Strait Islander flags should be permanently displayed outside both the Senate and House of Representatives chambers. The President, Senator Scott Ryan, wrote to me in response that "such matters are determined by the Senate itself, not the President. Any Senator is free to raise this matter in the Senate but I respectfully suggest it is further discussed within parties and between interested Senators before it is again brought to the chamber." That is, it is a matter for the Senate to determine. I predict that, in time, the flags of Indigenous Australia will be permanently displayed inside our nation's parliament—this would be a good and fair step forward.

We have come a long way on matters of symbolism in my lifetime. My good friend and the chairman of Uphold & Recognise, a group established to champion constitutional recognition, Sean Gordon, who belongs to the Wangkumarra of southern Queensland and the Barkindji from the New South Wales-Victoria border region, says he cannot believe how embedded the practice of acknowledging country has become—just as Aboriginal flags feature widely throughout our nation. We have added this to our national life without taking anything from anyone.

Delivering on national reconciliation

The purpose of national reconciliation is to move forward together as a modern nation. This goes beyond closing the gap and delivering symbolic changes. It is about structurally addressing the Great Australian Silence which has been manifested in paternalistic, blind, and destructive policymaking. The result of national reconciliation will be new institutions and new ways of doing things. There are effectively two policy approaches on the table today which could be deployed: Black Lives Matter and the Uluru Statement.

Black Lives Matter

I am not arguing the Black Lives Matter agenda should be deployed in Australia. Rather, it should be understood as it exists as a manifesto, however ill-defined and ill-suited to Australian conditions. To ignore it would be a mistake. During the 2020 Black Lives Matter protests in the United States, which led to marches in Australian cities, some argued it was an illegitimate imported campaign. Black Lives Matter started as a hashtag in 2013 following the death of an American police officer. It snowballed into a large semi-global movement during 2020, following the death of Minneapolis man George Floyd. The Parliamentary Library says of the Australian Black Lives Matter:

> In Australia, Black Lives Matter is probably best understood as a new phrase, slogan or campaign (rather than a new movement) for an existing set of concerns around the over incarceration of Aboriginal and Torres Strait Islander people and the high numbers of deaths in custody (police and prison). The global profile in 2020 has given these existing concerns within Australia a higher profile.

It seems true that Black Lives Matter in Australia, which does not appear to be formally organized, generally focuses on incarceration rates rather than anything broader. In the United States, the Black Lives Matter movement issued its platform in 2016 which sought to "end the war against black people", provide reparations for "past and continuing harms", and a range of policies to address disparity. The following year, in 2017, Black Lives Matter won the Sydney Peace Prize with the following citation:

> For building a powerful movement for racial equality, courageously reigniting a global conversation around state violence and racism. And for harnessing the potential of new platforms and power of people to inspire a bold movement for change at a time when peace is threatened by growing inequality and injustice.

Black Lives Matter advocates for extreme and absurd objectives like "defunding the police"—thereby damaging its credibility as a movement. In mid-2020, some American city mayors literally agreed to cut policing budgets. Yet Black Lives Matter co-founder and trained Marxist, Alicia Garza, tried to defend the objective by claiming it was about reprioritising resources:

> When we talk about defunding the police, what we're saying is 'invest in the resources that our communities need'. Are we willing to live in fear that our lives will be taken by police officers who are literally using their power in the wrong way? ... Or are we willing to adopt and absorb the fear of what it might mean to change our practices, which will ultimately lead to a better quality of life for everyone.

There can be no hiding the stated objective—"defund the police"—is wrong and very damaging to the movement. The idea of removing the police is not a credible solution in a liberal democracy with a rules-based order. While it is easy to dismiss the movement for going too far in places, the reality is the primary figures behind the Black Lives Matter movement are worse in Australia than they are in the United States. It has been a major issue facing the Indigenous community during my lifetime. Bob Hawke established a Royal Commission which reported in 1991 on deaths in custody. An increase in Indigenous deaths in custody during early 2021 shows more effort is needed.

Some of the Black Lives Matter protests resulted in nasty confrontations in the United States with innocent bystanders, such as in August 2020 in Washington DC, when people were asked to show their solidarity under threat of intimidation. The links between the Black Lives Matter movement and Marxist ideology or postmodernist attitudes towards power and authority are clear and embraced by the movement. But the links to postmodernism indicate the Black Lives Matter movement could never be placated because it is designed to overthrow the system of government.

That is what Marxism is designed to do: replace the liberal order. Postmodernism, which sits behind much of the Black Lives Matter content, is based on a belief that

> the social construction of knowledge is intimately tied to power, and that the more powerful culture creates the discourses that are granted legitimacy and determines what we consider to be truth and knowledge, in ways that maintain its dominance. It sees the world as a zero-sum power game and a conspiracy theory without individual conspirators.[17]

In crude summary, the consequence of adopting postmodernism and Marxism as a system of government would be pure anarchy. Black Lives Matter is radical, divisive, and will never deliver a unified Commonwealth. It isn't designed to do that. But it doesn't mean the underlying issues are illegitimate. The issues aren't going anywhere. Nor should they. Black Lives Matter had just 175 news mentions in 2016 which swelled to 2,806 in 2020 according to the Parliamentary Library. It is radical but it exists.

The Uluru Statement

The Uluru Statement of 26 May 2017 drew a line under the ten-year discussion John Howard kicked off on constitutional recognition in his last months in office. It ended the discussion on ornamental recognition and commenced the debate on functional recognition. The Uluru Statement is the Australian solution to the Australian problem. One view of Uluru comes from Pat Turner, who reminds us of the Stanner formula and says, "He termed this the Great Australian Silence. What he didn't say, but it was inferred, is that this structural silence means also shutting out Indigenous voices."[18] She says unlike New Zealand and Scandinavian nations, Australia has not established a formal consultative mechanism to engage Indigenous people. In arguing for Uluru's Voice, Turner says:

> I am not here to make you comfortable. Change does not happen when we are comfortable. It is also not comfortable for me. The life of an Indigenous person, struggling with the cry of our people to be heard, is not an easy one. And speaking out is rarely received by applause.

I came across the statement when I worked for the Business Council of Australia. It was championed within the council by Danny Gilbert—the Co-Chair of the Cape York Partnership and head of the law firm Gilbert and Tobin. Gilbert is a great friend of the Indigenous people—he has brought many people together in their service. I am one of his conscripts. Like many Australians, it took me some time to take in the statement. These days I let the pictures do the talking. After my election, I decided to hang the Uluru Statement in my Sydney electorate office. It hangs between two beautiful dot paintings on loan to me from Rachel Perkins. I have come to the view that Uluru is an important historic opportunity for our country—to level the playing field; to address past misdeeds; and deliver on a national reconciliation.

Uluru is a gift to the country. In many ways, it is an opportunity to consolidate Australia. It is an opportunity for our generation to break the cycle of rejection of Indigenous petitions and statements. It builds a mechanism for listening and we need these institutions to turn the tables on the past 250 years. There have been somewhat similar statements in the past. One of the most famous, which was mismanaged by the prior generations, was the Barunga Statement. In 1988, this statement was presented by the Yolngu people to Bob Hawke. It said there should be "A national elected Aboriginal and Islander organization to oversee Aboriginal and Islander affairs; a national system of land rights ... and we call on the Commonwealth Parliament to negotiate with us a Treaty recognising our prior ownership, continued occupation and sovereignty and affirming our human rights and freedom."

These are the same requests, in many respects, made in the Uluru Statement thirty years later. Our generation has a judgement to make—do we pursue Uluru, or do we let it go by the wayside and hope that the next generation has the stomach to address these issues? If we fail to deliver on Uluru, I do not believe there will be a better deal offered by the Indigenous people in the future. The Uluru Statement from the Heart reads as follows:

> Our Aboriginal and Torres Strait Islander tribes were the first sovereign Nations of the Australian continent and its adjacent islands, and possessed it under our own laws and customs. This our ancestors did, according to the reckoning of our culture, from the Creation, according to the common law from 'time immemorial', and according to science more than 60,000 years ago.
>
> This sovereignty is a spiritual notion: the ancestral tie between the land, or 'mother nature', and the Aboriginal and Torres Strait Islander peoples who were born therefrom, remain attached thereto, and must one day return thither to be united with our ancestors. This link is the basis of the ownership of the soil, or better, of sovereignty. It has never been ceded or extinguished, and co-exists with the sovereignty of the Crown.
>
> How could it be otherwise? That peoples possessed a land for sixty millennia and this sacred link disappears from world history in merely the last two hundred years? With substantive constitutional change and structural reform, we believe this ancient sovereignty can shine through as a fuller expression of Australia's nationhood.
>
> Proportionally, we are the most incarcerated people on the planet. We are not an innately criminal people. Our children are alienated from their families at unprecedented rates. This cannot be because we have no love for them. And our youth languish in

detention in obscene numbers. They should be our hope for the future.

These dimensions of our crisis tell plainly the structural nature of our problem. This is the torment of our powerlessness. We seek constitutional reforms to empower our people and take a rightful place in our own country. When we have power over our destiny our children will flourish. They will walk in two worlds and their culture will be a gift to their country. We call for the establishment of a First Nations Voice enshrined in the Constitution.

Makarrata is the culmination of our agenda: the coming together after a struggle. It captures our aspirations for a fair and truthful relationship with the people of Australia and a better future for our children based on justice and self-determination. We seek a Makarrata Commission to supervise a process of agreement-making between governments and First Nations and truth-telling about our history. In 1967 we were counted, in 2017 we seek to be heard. We leave base camp and start our trek across this vast country. We invite you to walk with us in a movement of the Australian people for a better future.

Uluru should be the ticket to a reconciled Australia; a consolidation of the Australian project. A chance to make good. I see Uluru as a very liberal idea, as does Stan Grant, who asks rhetorically, "How much more liberal can you get? A people that have been left out want to be part of liberal Australia."[19] It is an agenda for unity—for one Australia with different component parts. It says that Indigenous people want to be part of the Constitution of Australia. That is very much an endorsement of the Australian project. I see this as an opportunity to "complete the Constitution" as Tony Abbott said at Garma some years ago.

The great Liberal Party speechwriter (and my close friend) Paul Ritchie, and I have often remarked it was incredible that it took until 2016 for his book, *Faith, Love & Australia, the Conservative Case for Same Sex Marriage* to be published. Why hadn't someone else written this book a decade earlier? The essential argument in Ritchie's book is that widening the definition of marriage would strengthen families and the institution of marriage without taking anything away from any Australian. Upon agreeing to lead the Liberals and Nationals for Yes campaign, Ritchie presented me with a copy of his book. He wrote on the inside page "Andrew, I am excited we will be fighting alongside each other in the trenches. Let's win this. Paul Ritchie, August 2017."

I used Ritchie's book as my compass during the marriage campaign as it contained the key liberal and conservative arguments. I am now effectively proposing to sketch out the liberal and conservative arguments for delivering Uluru. There are certainly other arguments, I don't deny that, but I write this book as a sitting Senator seeking to win an argument. When the Uluru Statement was released, there was no strong liberal argument. I think there are effectively five key liberal and conservative arguments which should have accompanied the release of the statement, and they involve the following ideas:

- developed power
- legislative consultation
- honesty
- Liberal Party's capacity to deliver change
- pragmatism

First, the notion of devolved power. Uluru's Indigenous Voice, which I step through in detail in the following pages, is effectively a request for Canberra to devolve power to local communities. On the ground, this means allowing communities to make decisions on resourcing but also on advising the government. It means giving local community members authority to speak on behalf of Indigenous people on service delivery—rather than decisions made in Canberra or Macquarie Street.

Secondly, the Indigenous people are the only Australians who have a large number of special laws made for them based on race, which means we, as liberals, must provide a consultative mechanism. This is the only way to assure the value of equality in our liberal democracy. Native title, land rights, heritage protection, and a dozen standalone Acts of federal parliament provide for special laws for Indigenous people. It follows that the people for whom the laws are made should be given a say. That is the liberal democratic tradition. Anything else is illiberal.

Thirdly, honesty is a liberal virtue—it will set us all free by ending the history and culture wars. It will end the debate many conservatives dislike on statues. Embracing truth-telling allows for both sides of the story to be told. New statues can be erected. The assessment will cause some discomfort because Australia's success has too often been at the expense of Indigenous people. This is a truth we cannot hide. Australia is the twelfth largest economy on earth with a vibrant and diverse population which enjoys amongst the world's highest living standards and lifespans. Australia is a liberal democracy with robust public institutions. The truth about modern Australia has been honestly set out by historian and former Liberal MP, David Kemp. His principal thesis is that the triumph of Australian liberalism lays in the creation of a nation— admittedly with the failure to include Indigenous people. We have significant achievements in Australia—such as being early movers on universal suffrage—but Indigenous people were generally treated unfairly. That is something we can better acknowledge in the contemporary evaluation of Australia. The truth will build up the Australian project, not tear it down, because we are strong and good enough to make these important admissions.

Fourthly, our history shows the Liberals can carry the big, substantial changes. We are likely the only hope. The only chance to deliver. Unhelpfully, Liberals have written too few books on this and indeed on most subjects. Our record on delivering for Indigenous people has been good in parts, as this book has shown. Harold Holt delivered the most significant legal change to empower the Commonwealth to legislate for Indigenous people. Malcolm Fraser delivered land rights which today provide for more than half of Australia to be managed by Aboriginal people. The only party likely to deliver a successful referendum is the Liberal Party because we will pursue a unifying agenda—rather than a protest, or divisive approach, as would be the focus of the left. We are the only party to have successfully passed a referendum in relation to Indigenous Australians—with a 90% majority.

Fifthly, a better offer will not come along. The issues that were profiled in the Barunga Statement and the Uluru Statement won't go away. If there is a failure to deliver on the Uluru agenda, less cohesive solutions will be argued. If we fail to deliver substantially on Uluru, we can kiss goodbye to moderation, unity, and centrist positions. The Uluru Statement allows its elements to be delivered through various methods. It is not a prescriptive statement, which makes the efforts to oppose it even more troubling. It sets out principles but provides flexibility for policy delivery.

Is Uluru the number one priority?

It is clear from the public statements from Indigenous leaders across Australia that the Uluru Statement has a strong mandate from the 800,000 members of the Indigenous community. It is unreasonable to expect that every member of a community would agree with every idea in detail. Despite this, Aboriginal people from 200 different groups have shown a remarkable attraction to the Aboriginal flag. Most Aboriginal people support and identify with the Aboriginal flag.

My extensive travels across the State of New South Wales to meet with community members has provided me with further direct assurance that the idea of a Voice in particular is a high priority. Support is not universal; it is unreasonable to expect that everyone would agree with a single policy formulation. Certain members of the New South Wales Metropolitan Land Council have expressed a view that they will not support Uluru because there was insufficient consultation. But Grace Toomey, of the Wiradjuri in central New South Wales, a member of the New South Wales Aboriginal Land Council, whom I met in Dubbo, told me:

> The Voice to Parliament would be intended to provide meaningful input prior to the passage of legislation that impacts Aboriginal people. NSWALC supports constitutional reform to enshrine a Voice to Parliament as a priority. NSWALC called for further engagement with Aboriginal and Torres Strait Islander peoples, including Land Councils. This is needed to inform the design of the national Voice as well as local and regional Voices.

Leaders involved with the process, such as Langton and Pearson, are staunch advocates for a Voice. Their basis is their own statement, issued at Uluru in May 2017, where Pat Anderson said:

> Coming from all points of the southern sky, over 250 Delegates gathered at the 2017 First Nations National Constitutional Convention and today made a historic statement from the heart in hopes of improving the lives of future generations. The conversation at Uluru built on six months of discussions held around the country where Aboriginal and Torres Strait Islander peoples considered five options presented in the Referendum Council's discussion paper.

Noel Pearson says of the Voice:

> Ultimately, representation at the national level would be to enable all Aboriginal and Torres Strait Islander people to elect their representatives to represent their views to the Voice . . . Our summit has endorsed the idea that there should be one woman and one man selected from regions like Cape York . . . 50-50. We are very strong about having that sort of representation on this body.

In other words, the voices of Indigenous people have got to come through from the grassroots community, through the regional to the national.

Another Indigenous leader and professor of constitutional law, Megan Davis, who belongs to the Cobble Cobble people of southeast Queensland, says, "The Uluru process decided that a Voice to Parliament was the best way to embody that structural power so that the grassroots voices of the First Nation entity can be directly represented to the lawmakers and policymakers in Canberra." On the ground, Garry Trindall, of the Kamilaroi of the Queensland-New South Wales border region, who works for the Aboriginal Legal Service NSW/ACT in Coonamble, says, "In my opinion the people at the top lost contact with the grassroots people not by their choice but because of the system and workload. That's why I say we need to be represented by a voice from the communities at the grassroots, if possible the chairs of the working parties." Yet my colleague in the Senate, the Greens' Lidia Thorpe, says the Voice to Parliament is not a priority and the only thing that matters is establishing a treaty:

> We need a treaty. Aboriginal people in this country want peace. Let's deal with the crux of the problem that we have in this country. That is that we have never had an agreement with the First People to be here. Let's stop trying to divert to all these other things like changing the date and constitutional recognition and all these fluffy

things that do nothing. Let's deal with the hard issue.

This is a serious difference of opinion. One that cannot easily be reconciled. It appears to be a fairly isolated position but consistent with Thorpe's position at Uluru, where she said in 2017:

> We as sovereign First Nations people reject constitutional recognition. We do not recognise occupying power or their sovereignty, because it serves to disempower, and takes away our voice. We need to protect and preserve our sovereignty. We demand a sovereign treaty with an independent sovereign treaty commission, and appropriate funds allocated.

Thorpe's position, set out in her First Speech to the Senate, is simply that there should be a treaty before consideration is given to the question of constitutional recognition or creating voices. While this position may sound good to some people, this is neither a realistic position nor one which reflects reality or the maturity of the Australian project. Marcia Langton argues that Thorpe is not expressing a mainstream position: "It is a personal view, a very Victorian view. Totally unrepresentative of what Indigenous people want." It is also the view of Tasmanian Indigenous leader Michael Mansell, of the Palawa/Pinterrairer in northwest Tasmania), who argued in 2019 that a treaty is the only credible approach: "depending on what can be negotiated, a treaty could provide discrete Aboriginal communities with power over local policing (including customary law), local taxation, education, health, housing, road works and land use and planning."[20] Again, the bulk of these matters are handled by the States and are not things that the Commonwealth could deliver under our constitutional system. As explained below, treaties are generally about land and financial settlements. These are addressed in Australia—however inadequately—through land rights and native title legislation, which have led to more than half of the continent being returned to Indigenous Australians. The next pages evaluate the three core elements of the Uluru Statement: voice, treaty, and truth. (While the Statement itself does not mention the word treaty, it has been widely used in the marketing of the Statement.)

Voice

My inquiries as to levels of support for this body suggest that while it means different things to different Indigenous people, it is widely supported. The idea of a formally constituted body or voice has been around for decades. In a crude form, the Holt reform of the Aboriginal Affairs Council after the referendum of 1967 was an early attempt at hearing Indigenous voices. Stanner and 'Nugget' Coombs engaged with leaders of the day—such as Charles Perkins—although theirs was, of course, a paternalistic solution and not a Voice. Marcia Langton maintains that "the Voice developed from the NAC." The Whitlam government established the National Aboriginal Conference in 1973. It was abolished by the Fraser government and replaced by a new body of the same name with thirty-five elected members. Ian Viner told the National Press Club in 1977 that the National Aboriginal Conference would hold discussions "in which members will debate and express an Australia-wide Aboriginal view on long term goals which the government should pursue, programmes it should adopt and priorities for expenditure."[21]

The National Aboriginal Conference led discussions on a makarrata in the 1970s and 1980s until it was abolished by the Hawke Government in 1985. It was the body that the 1981-83

Senate's makarrata inquiry considered best placed to represent Indigenous people in a treaty-making process. The second recommendation of that inquiry's report was that "the NAC should take the opportunity offered to it by the government to seek re-establishment of an independent statutory basis with an increase in membership, so as to allow for more effective representation of the Aboriginal people." Sadly, Hawke's minister, Clyde Holding, said in 1985 that the National Aboriginal Conference was beset with "financial administration" problems. The next years were spent by the Hawke administration deciding what its replacement should be.

In 1987, a minister in the Hawke government, Gerry Hand, said it would establish an Aboriginal and Torres Strait Islander Commission. This would combine both representative and executive roles, and "so allay the criticism that decision-making power over Aboriginal affairs had never been fully given to Aboriginal people". ATSIC was not supported by the Coalition. Some Senators said it would be a 'black parliament'. Nevertheless, the ATSIC bills were passed in late 1989, two years after they were first introduced.

ATSIC had two functions, which were performed by an elected arm and an administrative arm. The elected arm had eighteen commissioners, drawn from the thirty-five regions. The administrative arm employed 1,200 staff, who administered the programmes as determined by the elected arm. ATSIC was many things. It was more than an advisory group. It was involved in spending and distributing money. Paul Keating's adviser and biographer, Don Watson, said, "No one in Canberra was in much doubt that under ATSIC, a lot of the money was not getting to the places it was needed."[22]

The Minister responsible for ATSIC for most of the Howard era, Philip Ruddock, sought to improve ATSIC's administrative arrangements. Ruddock announced a separation of policy and expenditure in April 2003, explaining: "From 1 July 2003, all individual funding decisions concerning programmes delivered by ATSIC will be made by officers of the administrative arm." Under the Westminster system of government, ministers normally decide policy and officials implement it. ATSIC is unique in that it effectively exercised ministerial policymaking powers. Ruddock's statement continued:

> There has been no separation between this role and decisions to enter contracts or allocate funds to particular organizations or individuals, resulting in the potential for perceived or actual conflict of interest. This is contrary to good governance. The micro-management focus on ATSIC's own spending has also distracted the elected arm from more significant policy issues.[23]

Ruddock was subsequently promoted to become Attorney-General in October 2003. The governance issues were not resolved. Peter Costello wrote in his memoir:

> The Commission was highly politicised and highly factionalised. There were financial irregularities. The final blow was when the chairman of the Commission was charged with rape, brought by an Aboriginal woman, over events that occurred many years before. ATSIC was paralysed and the public had no confidence in it. Nor did I.[24]

Ultimately, ATSIC was abolished by John Howard and Ruddock's successor, Amanda Vanstone. In April 2004, Howard said, "We believe very strongly that the experiment in separate representation, elected representation, for Indigenous people has been a failure. We will not replace ATSIC with an alternative body." ATSIC had enormous problems. There is no doubt about this question. Yet there are mixed views about its abolition. Philip Ruddock says ATSIC was abolished when it could have been fixed, explaining:

> On abolition it was a Government decision while Amanda (Vanstone) was Minister. I was a member of the government. The problem with the organization's management issues was how they were resolved particularly if dismissal is not possible.

Malcolm Fraser was "dismayed when in 2005 the Howard government abolished ATSIC without replacing it with anything else."[25] Since 2005, there has been no formal elected structure to represent Indigenous people to Canberra for the first time since Fraser.

Constitutional recognition and the Voice

The Voice is the brainchild of Noel Pearson and his influential Cape York Institute for Policy and Leadership. Pearson's proposal would fill a gap created a decade earlier. Pearson said in 2016 that "I was adamant that any constitutional recognition of Indigenous peoples must be substantive and practical—it must provide a solution to the racial discrimination of the past, or else it was not worth pursuing." That this became the position embraced by Indigenous people in the Uluru Statement owes much, Langton maintains, to "the advocacy of Noel Pearson and his outstanding essay a *Rightful Place*."[26] Despite this, a Voice was merely a sidenote of the constitutional reform debate of a fruitless decade from 2007-2017. During the decade between 2010 and 2020, there were four reviews commissioned by prime ministers. One by Julia Gillard, another by Tony Abbott, and two during

Malcolm Turnbull's tenure. The various reviews and conceptions of Indigenous recognition in the Constitution did not deal with the question of a Voice until the Uluru Statement was tabled on 26 May 2017 and incorporated into the Referendum Council report to Turnbull and Shorten in June 2017.

Pearson set out the Voice in his landmark Quarterly Essay, *A Rightful Place*. The 2014 Cape York position argues that a new body should be established in the Constitution to provide formal consultation:

> Properly drafted, constructed and run, this new constitutional body could represent a significant and exciting reform that would provide Indigenous people an important and guaranteed platform to be heard within the formal mechanisms of Parliament. This could create the machinery for a constructive partnership and set the basis for a fairer relationship into the future.

Pearson included his Voice concept in a speech to mark the fiftieth anniversary dinner of *The Australian* newspaper:

> Our nation is in three parts. There is our ancient heritage, written in the continent and the original culture painted on its land and seascapes. There is our British inheritance, the structures of government and society transported from the United Kingdom fixing its foundations in the ancient soil. There is our multicultural achievement: a triumph of immigration that brought together the gifts of peoples and cultures from all over the globe—forming one indissoluble Commonwealth.

This is the position that Pearson uses to set out his view that the Commonwealth Constitution is not the place to have a detailed preamble set out in the constitution—which is a practical rule book. Pearson did not set out a detailed model in his pivotal Quarterly Essay. The Referendum Council report of 2017 acknowledged that the Voice was not a new idea, and had been widely supported during the Council's community dialogue. Its final report stated:

> The Voice was the most endorsed singular option for constitutional alteration. A constitutionally entrenched Voice appealed to Aboriginal and Torres Strait Islander communities because of the history of poor or non-existent consultation with communities by the Commonwealth. Consultation is either very superficial or it is more meaningful, but then wholly ignored.

Accordingly, the Referendum Council recommended that the Constitution be amended to provide for a "representative body that gives Aboriginal and Torres Strait Islander First Nations a Voice to the Commonwealth Parliament." But, as Malcolm Turnbull explains, the Referendum Council did not deliver the required detail. No drafting for an amendment was forthcoming. It was a big failure of the Council to offer no drafting whatsoever and, in doing so, the Referendum Council effectively reverted to the 2014 Pearson position which was just an idea, rather than a detailed proposal for an amendment to the Constitution. The prime minister and the opposition leader tasked the Referendum Council with recommending specific changes to the Constitution, but it failed to deliver anything more than an idea that could be turned into an amendment to the Constitution, if someone else wanted to work out how to do it.

The Voice in Uluru

The Uluru Statement was issued shortly before the Referendum Council report. The position on the Voice put at Uluru was simple: "We call for the establishment of a First Nations Voice enshrined in the Constitution." That provided considerable scope for the Voice to be formulated. Uluru was not prescriptive about the form a Voice could take or about how it would be enshrined in the Constitution. The argument for the Voice was set out by human rights advocate Pat Anderson, of the Alyawarre from the Alice Springs region of the Northern Territory, together with Megan Davis and Noel Pearson in *The Australian* in May 2017. They explained the death of ornamental recognition and the birth of the Voice as follows:

> We heard unequivocally that mere symbolism in the Constitution is not desired by Aboriginal and Torres Strait Islander people but rather practical and pragmatic reform that could make a difference to the lives of Australia's original and most disadvantaged group. The regional dialogues said they wanted to take responsibility and control over their lives and decisions made about them. These decisions are taken by politicians and public servants in Canberra and the capital cities.

The Voice had become the preferred form of constitutional recognition amongst the Indigenous leadership. Uluru turned one man's idea, expressed three years earlier, into the formal position of Australia's Indigenous peoples. This included a mandate from the communities consulted during the dialogues leading into the Uluru meeting in mid-2017.

There were two reasons why the prime minister at the time, Malcolm Turnbull, did not accept the recommendation for a Voice. First, he simply didn't agree with the premise that there should be an Indigenous representative body in the Constitution. The second reason is that he thought it had no chance at a referendum. This latter reason is perhaps a reflection of the scar tissue he bore from the defeat of the republic referendum in 1999. Turnbull had led the Australian Republican Movement during the referendum.

Turnbull was clearly frustrated that the Referendum Council, which he had appointed, had failed to deliver a proposed constitutional amendment as it had been asked to do, and he continued to argue that the lack of detail was a material problem well after leaving office. Turnbull writes in his memoir:

> The Uluru Statement from the Heart left me deeply conflicted. It was a beautiful piece of poetry, a cry for a say, a cry for agency, for respect. But it contained no detail at all about how such a Voice would be designed . . . in practical terms, such a Voice would effectively evolve into a third chamber.[27]

On 26 October 2017, Turnbull formally rejected the Referendum Council's recommendation about the Voice. His statement read:

> The Turnbull Government has carefully considered the Referendum Council's call to amend the Constitution to provide for a national Indigenous representative assembly to constitute a 'Voice to Parliament'. The Government does not believe such an addition to our national representative institutions is either desirable or capable of winning acceptance in a referendum. A constitutionally enshrined additional representative assembly for which only Indigenous Australians could vote for or serve in is inconsistent with this fundamental principle. It would inevitably become seen as a third chamber of Parliament.[28]

In retrospect Turnbull has stuck with this position:

> And I did not think that was a good idea to put in the Constitution. I might say, I also believed, and I say this with the experience of someone who knows what it's like to lose a constitutional referendum, I don't think it has any prospect of being successful in a referendum. It's literally doomed because it would be opposed strongly. And the lesson from constitutional referenda is that unless you get virtually everyone to agree with it, you can't get it up.[29]

His conclusion about referendums is blunt:

> Referendums are very, very easy to defeat—the track record shows that. I have written about this in my memoir and in other books, but in a nutshell the consequence of compulsory voting is that people with a low level of interest in and information about the question are obliged to vote and they will inevitably default

to a No vote. So that builds in a substantial conservative vote. It has followed, therefore, that the only referendums which succeed are those in which there is very little opposition. The last mildly controversial referendum which was approved was in fact in 1946. So you need to get overwhelming support and minimal opposition. That's the history. Clearly a referendum that was stated to address reconciliation which was defeated would be very damaging. Where you want to be is as we were in 1967 with near universal support.[30]

While Turnbull suggested a Voice to Parliament would not succeed, the idea was referred to a parliamentary committee to be co-chaired by Senator Patrick Dodson and Julian Leeser MP. Paradoxically, this was both a setback and an avenue for the Voice to find a new political life.

The third chamber

Uluru never included the words 'assembly', 'body', or 'chamber'. These terms were invented by others in their advocacy against the Voice. The claim that it would become a 'third chamber' did the most damage to support for the Voice amongst liberals and conservatives. Where did this tag come from? On 27 May 2017, the Uluru Statement was read aloud at Uluru in central Australia. Two days later, the Deputy Prime Minister, Barnaby Joyce, said that it was unwise to "ask for something that will not be supported by the Australian people, such as another chamber in politics or something that sits beside or above the Senate, that idea just won't fly." By the time the Referendum Council reported on 30 June, the Voice was in big trouble and Turnbull's response was inevitable. In late June 2017, the Turnbull government was under immense internal pressure on the issue of same-sex marriage. The 'splash' in *The Australian* on 27 June read:

The new clash looms as some Liberals consider a conscience vote in Parliament that could legislate gay marriage by the end of this year, despite a warning from Tony Abbott that the government must hold to its pledge of a popular vote to decide the social reform.

The lead story in *The Australian* on 28 June opened with:

Malcolm Turnbull faces a test of his leadership as a bloc of Liberal MPs push to legislate for same sex marriage before the next election, in a move that threatens the Coalition agreement with the Nationals and risks a civil war inside the partyroom.[31]

During this year, I was engaged first as acting federal director of the Liberal Party from May until August, and then as national director of the Liberals & Nationals for Yes campaign from August until November. The issue of same-sex marriage was toxic within the Coalition. Labor had blocked the plebiscite bills in the Senate and, therefore, the same-sex marriage issue looked like it could dog the government until the 2019 election. Some Nationals had made it publicly clear that any departure from the 2016 election policy of a plebiscite on marriage would result in the end of the Coalition agreement. Others had proposed a private member's bill to bring on a conscious vote. The Government had a one seat majority and mismanagement of any single issue could drive the government into opposition.

One senior minister, Christopher Pyne, had been secretly taped saying that he expected marriage equality would soon be delivered. This was a fractious issue which limited the government's capacity to deal with other challenging issues like constitutional reform proposals. Ultimately, a postal survey asking Australians their opinion on changing the law to allow same-sex couples to marry was conducted. It indicated the majority of people supported the change, and this led to legalisation of same-sex marriage in

Australia. So there was a lot going on in the month after the Uluru Statement was delivered. My judgement is that Malcolm Turnbull was looking for a solution to marriage equality and the events of the day were such that a second highly fractious issue could not be addressed. Turnbull campaigned in favour of the proposed change to the *Marriage Act*. It was a policy change he had long sought and he personally launched the Liberals & Nationals for Yes campaign. The public opposition of the leader of the Nationals to the Voice made it very hard to open a front on the Voice—even if Turnbull had wanted to. Adopting the 'third chamber' language placated the Nationals and allowed division within the government to be contained.

A 'third chamber' is a witty and easily understood concept to kill off support. The reality is that the only thing many people have heard about a Voice is that it would be a 'third chamber'. Malcolm Turnbull said in his response to the Uluru Statement that the Voice would be an "additional representative assembly" when it was not necessarily going to be. A third illiberal chamber could be imagined as a House of Parliament with only Aboriginal membership—there to consider all manner of bills and policies. This was a fiction. In the end, Joyce admitted he had made a "mistake" and should not have said the Voice was a third chamber: "If I got it wrong, I apologise. I apologise. There you go. Unreservedly."[32] But the damage was done—the conservative solution put forward by the Indigenous leadership had little support amongst liberals and conservatives. It was perceived to be even worse than a preamble or a bill of rights. It was a shallow response to a historically significant statement.

Dodson-Leeser revival

The parliamentary inquiry supported by Turnbull and Shorten meant the Voice had a chance at a revival. The Joint Select Committee on Constitutional Recognition relating to Aboriginal and Torres Strait Islander Peoples (Dodson-Leeser Committee) looked in detail at models, including the type of constitutional amendments which Turnbull had expected the Referendum Council to deliver. Dodson-Leeser made two key recommendations on the Voice. In November 2018, the committee's bipartisan report delivered a consensus position which reflects well on both Dodson and Leeser.

The first recommendation from the committee was to fill in the details from Uluru by conducting a process of 'co-design'. Co-design by Indigenous people and the government would involve looking at how each of the national, regional, and local elements of the Voice would work in practice, and how they would interconnect. The report said this must be "conducted by a group comprising a majority of Aboriginal and Torres Strait Islander communities and organizations across Australia, including remote, regional and urban communities."[33] Together, these communities and the government would look at structure, membership, functions, and operation. Models would be developed during the next parliament.

The second recommendation was that "following a process of co-design, the Australian Government consider, in a deliberative and timely manner, legislative, executive and constitutional options to establish the Voice."[34] These bipartisan recommendations laid a foundation for achieving the Voice.

Same-sex marriage was dealt with during the Turnbull government and there was a new prime minister, Scott Morrison, from August 2018. The Morrison government accepted the Leeser-Dodson report's recommendations and promised to commission the co-design process which was recommended. The government's policy statement for the 2019 election said:

> We are listening to the recommendations of the bi-partisan Joint Select Committee . . . But there needs to be more work done on what model we take to a referendum and what a Voice to parliament would be—which is why we are funding a consultation process with Aboriginal and Torres Strait Islander Australians. This process will develop a question for a referendum and what a referendum will deliver—because no one can answer what a Voice to parliament actually is at the moment. To deliver on this recommendation, the Morrison Government is providing $7.3 million for the comprehensive co-design of models to improve local and regional decision making and options for constitutional recognition. This work will commence immediately to provide a model and pathway to a successful referendum.[35]

Accordingly, the 2019-20 Budget contained funding to support the process of co-design. The Minister for Indigenous Affairs, Nigel Scullion, said in April 2019 that "still after all this time, [the Voice] is five letters. We would like to understand what a Voice is before we put it to the Australian people. So this process is to put some meat on the bones, so we can all actually understand what that is."[36] In March 2020, Morrison gave a speech in which he said:

> We support the process of co-design of the Voice because if we are going to change the lives of Aboriginal and Torres Strait Islander peoples on the ground, we need their buy-in to the matters and policies that affect them. The Committee did not make recommendations as to the legal form of the Voice, constitutional or legislation. It recommended considering this matter after the process of co-design is complete and that's what we are doing. We support finalising co-design first.

This reaffirmed the prime minister's commitment to the Leeser-Dodson report which again highlights the significance of the work done by Dodson and Leeser. It brought the Voice back from the political grave.

An Indigenous minister for Indigenous Australia

Following his victory in the election of May 2019, Scott Morrison took the historic step of appointing Australia's first Indigenous Minister for Indigenous Australians, Ken Wyatt. Wyatt received a phone call from the prime minister just after the election. He recalls:

> I was hanging up a tablecloth on the Hills Hoist clothesline when the phone rang and the Prime Minister's name came up. I answered the phone with, "Good morning, Prime Minister." I thought that he was offering me my previous portfolio.

The prime minister was calling with an historic opportunity for Wyatt:

> Instead, he said, "I want to thank you for your support for senior Australians, the work in the aged-care sector and Indigenous health. I would like to offer you the position of Minister for Indigenous Australians." It took me a full two minutes to answer him. In those two minutes, the emotions of our story, as Indigenous Australians, welled up in me. It's hard to express what I actually felt and what it meant to me at the time.

This appointment created an expectation and a good deal of pressure on Wyatt as a minister who would be expected to deliver like no other in our history as the first Aboriginal person to be the minister. One month after Wyatt's appointment, the former Chief Justice of the High Court, Murray Gleeson, said a Voice was certainly not a third chamber. During the address, Gleeson said, "What is proposed is a Voice to Parliament, not a Voice in Parliament . . . It has the merit that it is substantive, and not merely ornamental." Gleeson's address helped discredit the third chamber tag intellectually—it also set out a workable framework for designing a Voice within our constitutional arrangements:

> The structure, composition and functions of the proposed representative body would be determined, and susceptible to

change, by legislation of the federal Parliament. What would appear in the Constitution would be the minimum requirements necessary to guarantee its continued existence and its essential characteristics.

In other words, the Constitution could set out an obligation for the national government to consult with Indigenous Australians through a Voice established by the parliament.

Voice co-design

The work of co-designing the Voice would do two things: put 'meat on the bones' of the original idea and provide for majority Indigenous design. In November 2019, Wyatt appointed the Senior Advisory Group for co-design with Marcia Langton and Tom Calma as co-chairs. He said the group "will advise me on options for models that will ensure that Indigenous Australians are heard at all levels of government—local, state and federal. They will be tasked with forming a National Co-Design Group and a Local/ Regional Co-Design Group."

The Senior Advisory Group's interim report, which was publicly released in January 2021, dealt with the practical elements of how a national voice, regional voice, and local voice could work. This includes the structure of voice architecture but also the arrangements for selecting members of each. It did not discuss the question of constitutional arrangements, which the minister had stipulated was not within the group's terms of reference.

Assembling a Voice

What is a Voice? A Voice is a reasonably simple idea. It has developed in a way that reveals two key features: consultation and bottom-up control. Within communities, it would provide a formalised structure to provide feedback to the government but also to influence the community's service delivery. It would not direct activities or authorise spending. The mechanism has been described by Danny Gilbert as "recognition at once both symbolic and substantive. It's a call for an end to the silence in the pages of our Constitution—our rulebook of national governance. It's a call for us to listen to them."[37] There are effectively three components required to deliver a Voice to Indigenous people: first, Indigenous voices need to be heard at the local and regional level; secondly, they need to be heard at the national level; and, thirdly, in addition to the legal machinery to enable them to speak at these levels, there needs to be a constitutional guarantee that Indigenous voices shall be heard when the Commonwealth exercises its powers in relation to Indigenous affairs.

A local voice

A local voice would empower local communities with the capacity to advise government on local issues and influence resourcing. Dozens of local voice structures would be required to allow the diverse groups of Indigenous Australians to have their say. One of the most enlightening trips of my parliamentary career was a visit to the central west of New South Wales in November 2020. I travelled through Walgett, Coonamble, Brewarrina, and Burke. Representation to the government is an issue which is regularly raised with me. Since ATSIC was abolished in 2005, many splinter groups have formed to represent the extremely diverse regional voices of Indigenous Australia. As I travelled through these parts with my friend, Sean Gordon, we had discussions with people on land councils, tribal councils, municipal councils, and the Murdi Paaki Regional Authority, which represents sixteen Aboriginal communities in western New South Wales.

Murdi Paaki allows Aboriginal people living in the region to attend meetings of the local community working groups, become voting members, and elect a chairperson. In some communities, it is supported, in other towns, it hasn't worked. For example, Burke pulled out of Murdi Paaki to establish its own organization called Maranguka. One model for a local Voice is for two members from each of these groups (male and female) would be appointed to a state body. This would advise government departments and agencies on service delivery and lead engagement with local and state government.

There are similar models across the country, some are set up by communities, others have been established under statute. For example, the Torres Strait Regional Authority exists under a law of the Commonwealth. It has twenty board members who are each elected to represent a ward—an island or discrete community. It supports economic development, protection of cultural heritage, and health and community services. The view on the ground in communities that I have visited in New South Wales is clear about the concept.

Brad Gordon, who belongs to the Wangkumarra of southern Queensland and the Barkindji of the border region between New South Wales and Victoria, is a passionate local from Brewarrina in western New South Wales. He says:

> I want for my community and people to not just be heard by parliament, but to be listened to by our politicians and that our pleads and cries for help do not fall on deaf ears and that the

words of our political leaders is followed by genuine action that leads to better outcomes for our mob. Our people are suffering, our despair is real, our disparity is measurable and unacceptable. It is time to give rise to a model that gives voice to our people on the ground to develop our own solutions based on our own traditional practices.

Alistair Ferguson, who belongs to the Ngemba of the Barwon-Darling region, the Wiradjuri of central New South Wales, the Yorta Yorta of the Murray-Goulburn region, and the Kullila of southeast Queensland), is the executive director of Burke's Maranguka community hub. He says:

> Maranguka, meaning caring for others in Ngemba language is a Community Hub that works alongside the people of Bourke. Maranguka is a grassroots tool for all our people to shape and determine our future. We need the right mix of services delivered at the right times to stop our people from falling between the gaps. As a community we need to be empowered to take greater self-responsibility in coordinating services and caring for our own.

Another view comes from Lillian Moseley, whose heritage includes Dunghutti of the Macleay Valley in northern New South Wales, Birpai of the State's mid-north coast, Worimi of eastern Port Stephens, and Yuin of the south coast. She is an elder who lives in Kempsey. She says:

> The voice of the grassroots people is not getting through to the elite leaders who are not listening to the community. There is no real connection from the State or federal level directly with the people at the local level, from the people themselves. I am setting up a model for the Kempsey area, the Justice Reinvestment Committee, which is a Voice. You can't speak on the behalf of other tribal groups, so if you don't get it right from the start, you'll never get it right.

In essence, this is about ensuring community input in service delivery. It's about getting kids to school on the bus or providing antenatal services to pregnant women with community input and control. From the bottom up, a Voice can deliver a form of community decision-making. Or perhaps it is better described as formalising a policy of self-determination. My Indigenous constituents present a clear consensus that more local control of community services is needed. It puts the concept of *doing with* rather than *doing to* into practice. This formula has been eloquently set out by Andrea Mason of the Ngaanyatjarra in Western Australia's Warburton Ranges and the Karonie of the Kalgoorlie region, who explains that "it's about us, and anything that's about us needs to be shaped by us." One particular model, which is considered in the Langton-Calma interim report, is described as providing a "building blocks" approach where local groups can come together and amalgamate into a broader district group representing different parts of Australia. These groups would then engage directly with the national Voice which in turn works with the national parliament. The local Voice could, in fact, occupy positions on the national voice.

A national voice

A national Voice would provide a new way for the national parliament to engage with Indigenous people. This need is particularly acute because the relationship between the two is unique. The only times when the parliament has used its powers to make special laws for the people of a particular race is when it has made laws with respect to Indigenous people. Noel Pearson, the driver of the Voice, said in 2015 that "the substantive constitutional amendment guaranteeing the Indigenous Voice in Indigenous affairs has the potential to instigate a profound shift in the way political conversations with respect to Indigenous affairs take place."[38] At a minimum, a Voice could be deployed to consult with the people whom the parliament has determined require these special laws.

Former Business Council of Australia president, Graham Bradley, noted that "Its task would be to provide publicly accessible advice, tabled in Parliament, for legislators to consider in relation to proposed laws and policies affecting Indigenous Australians."[39]

There is a clear agenda for a national Voice. There are at least four things it could do tomorrow.

First, it could advise on legislation which is made specifically for Indigenous Australians—such as the *Native Title Act*. In December 2020, the parliament considered an amendment to this Act. As part of the briefing materials provided to parliamentarians or as part of the Senate committee process, there could have been a summary of advice on the bill from the Voice. There could be simple advice from the Voice on each proposed amendment to relevant laws— just like a briefing from a government department. This is a gap in our process which I see as a legislator. I can also understand the perspective of the communities with whom I have met.

Secondly, it could provide binding advice on the use of the Aboriginal flag, assuming at some stage the Commonwealth is able to agree with Harold Thomas to acquire the flag, it will need an appropriate home. The flag's usage and protocols will need to be maintained properly. Given its historical usage as a flag of protest, it will surely fit into a structure like a representative Indigenous body rather than being buried in a department or Canberra agency.

Thirdly, it could fulfill the role of cultural adviser. As the

Australia Council for the Arts has explained, "There is no national peak body working across art forms to promote the rights of First Nations artists and cultural custodians to champion First Nations arts and cultures . . . For decades, numerous reports, inquiries and campaigns have highlighted issues of misuse and misappropriation of First Nations arts and culture and the idea of a national peak body to help address them." A detailed mandate for a cultural authority was set out by Terri Janke in her 2008 Wentworth Lecture. To facilitate greater integration of Indigenous culture into the parliamentary processes, a cultural adviser could be drawn upon for events including the Opening of Parliament each year. In the next chapter, I propose changes to the Opening of Parliament to ensure there is a stronger link to Indigenous culture. This would be appropriate as we seek to embrace Indigenous culture in our national life.

Fourthly, it could be a collector, aggregator, and analyst of data in conjunction with the Productivity Commission. It could provide advice to the government about expenditure generally in the Indigenous policy portfolio, but it could also offer a view on the successes and failures of the local and regional Voice programmes. This is a large industry which has not performed strongly. More than $33 billion was spent on Indigenous programmes in 2015-16, according to the Productivity Commission. In a ground-breaking study in 2020, the commission reported:

> Some agencies have developed extensive evaluation guidelines, strategies and systems—others have very little in comparison. The level of transparency of evaluation activities across the Commonwealth is low and there is limited data on how much is spent on evaluation. Recent reports have indicated that evaluation practice among Commonwealth agencies is lacking and should be improved.

In October 2020, the Productivity Commission released its Indigenous Evaluation Strategy. It sets out its objective as follows:

> Evaluations should contribute to a high-quality, useful and accessible body of evidence that government and Aboriginal and Torres Strait Islander people, organizations and communities have confidence to use when designing, modifying and implementing policies and programs.

This puts Indigenous people at the centre of the process. It seeks credible, useful evidence as part of the planning process, which must be transparent and ethical in its collection. The strategy is intended to be applied in the departments and various bodies established by the government. It would make sense for the national Voice to co-own this process.

The national Voice must build strong engagement with the federal parliament and should be folded into the highly successful parliamentary committee system. In this way, the Voice could establish a permanent two-way dialogue on a proactive and reactive basis and could cement a revolution in engagement between policymakers and Indigenous Australia. In addition to a formal statutory Voice committee, the Langton-Calma interim report sets out a very practical role for the national Voice to formally table advice to parliament and provide statements of advice on relevant legislation. There are more examples to draw upon as time passes. At the time of writing, the South Australian government is developing a Voice to Parliament under Steven Marshall.

Constitutional arrangements

To keep faith with the Uluru Statement, the principle of consultation on laws and policies affecting Indigenous people should be enshrined in the Constitution. There have been at least three attempts to draft the constitutional amendment required by the Uluru Statement in recent years. Each of the models has been developed in good faith to deliver on the statement. Naturally, they differ in levels of detail and ambition. I make these assessments as a parliamentarian without legal training whilst noting my clear preference for minimal changes to the words in our Constitution.

Twomey 2015

In 2015, the first model emerged thanks to University of Sydney constitutional expert Anne Twomey. Her model was set out in *The Conversation* in 2015. This detailed model is as follows:

60A (1) There shall be an Aboriginal and Torres Strait Islander body, to be called the [insert appropriate name, perhaps drawn from an Aboriginal or Torres Strait Islander language], which shall have the function of providing advice to the Parliament and the Executive Government on matters relating to Aboriginal and Torres Strait Islander peoples.

(2) The Parliament shall, subject to this Constitution, have power to make laws with respect to the composition, roles, powers and procedures of the [body].

(3) The Prime Minister [or the Speaker/President of the Senate] shall cause a copy of the [body's] advice to be tabled in each House of Parliament as soon as practicable after receiving it.

(4) The House of Representatives and the Senate shall give consideration to the tabled advice of the [body] in debating proposed laws with respect to Aboriginal and Torres Strait Islander peoples.[40]

In simple terms, it contains four requirements: (1) to establish a body; (2) to put it under the parliament's control; (3) to require advice to be tabled in parliament; and, (4) to require the two chambers to consider the tabled advice. Twomey has described the

2015 model in the following terms:

> It was deliberately drafted to avoid 'third House of Parliament' claims, which is why it is so distressing that they were still made, without any foundation. The obligation to consider advice was confined to 'tabled advice', so that it was clear what the advice was, and there was no obligation to consider anything unless advice had been provided and tabled at the time the bill was debated. This meant that there was no ability to delay or frustrate Parliament by withholding advice or not providing it promptly. The obligation to consider tabled advice only arose with respect to debates on the relatively narrow category of 'proposed laws with respect to Aboriginal and Torres Strait Islander people' (as opposed to the broader category of 'matters relating to Aboriginal and Torres Strait Islander peoples', about which advice could be given, but in relation to which there was no obligation of consideration). The obligation was confined to consideration during debate upon proposed laws, rendering it non-justiciable because it would be part of the internal proceedings of the Houses."[41]

But despite Twomey's assertion about avoiding a 'third house' with this model, her 2015 model was rejected by Turnbull as part of his government's position on the Uluru Statement, seemingly because it appeared to be 'a third chamber'. In my opinion, while the model is clear, it is very detailed which creates more risk than a model with fewer words and fewer provisions.

Anderson-Davis-Pearson 2018

In their submission to the 2018 Inquiry, Pat Anderson, Megan Davis, Noel Pearson, and others proposed a variation on the Twomey 2015 model as follows:

Section 129 The First Nations Voice

1. There shall be a First Nations Voice.

2. The First Nations Voice shall present its views to Parliament and

the Executive on matters relating to Aboriginal and Torres Strait Islander peoples.

3. The Parliament shall, subject to this Constitution, have power to make laws with respect to the composition, functions, powers and procedures of the First Nations Voice.[42]

Although this is similar to the Twomey 2015 model, I am more open minded about this model because of its focus and simplicity. It avoids the issues in the Twomey 2015 model, namely that it was too detailed and that the 'tabling provision' was problematic. Without the tabling provision, it is simpler and cleaner than Twomey 2015, partly for the very simple reason that it contains fewer words and fewer provisions. However, although this model has its strengths, it may still fall foul of the 'third chamber' objection because it establishes in the Constitution a body which would "present its views".

Twomey 2020

The third model was also drafted by Professor Twomey. In which a new section 127, which I call Twomey 2020, would set out the following requirement:

127. The Commonwealth shall make provision for Aboriginal and Torres Strait Islander peoples to be heard by the Commonwealth regarding proposed laws and other matters with respect to Aboriginal and Torres Strait Islander affairs, and the Parliament may make laws to give effect to this provision.[43]

This Twomey 2020 model is a serious response to the 'third chamber' narrative which, at the same time, delivers on the Uluru request for constitutional enshrinement. Twomey stands by both of her models and describes the context for this second option as follows: Even though the 2015 model is my personal preference, I accept that in politics it is often necessary to be flexible and to seek to achieve the same outcome by different means."[44] She says of her second amendment:

> It would provide a constitutional 'anchor' for the proposition that Aboriginal and Torres Strait Islander peoples must be heard by the Commonwealth regarding proposed laws (i.e. bills in Parliament) and other matters (such as policy matters concerning the exercise of executive power). This goes further than the notion of a 'Voice', by focusing on the response to that Voice—being heard. It is through that voice being heard that there is active constitutional recognition, rather than mere words on the page of the Constitution. The provision would also create a constitutional obligation to act, but would do so in a manner that is non-justiciable, avoiding litigation. Instead, the proposed amendment would empower Parliament to give effect to this obligation, but it could also be given effect by Executive action, such as administrative mechanisms for consultation with the Commonwealth Government. It would be up to the Commonwealth to make legislative or executive provision, or both, to give effect to the obligation . . .

> The primary difference from the 2015 model is that the 2020 one is less prescriptive of the mechanism by which Aboriginal and Torres Strait Islander peoples are to be heard. It leaves the mechanism to the Commonwealth to determine.

Twomey 2020 leaves it to the parliament to resolve everything, thereby avoiding the very legitimate concerns of constitutional conservatives that detailed amendments are risky, especially in the age of the High Court's *Love* judgement. Given the difficulty of achieving constitutional reform in Australia, Twomey 2020 is the model most likely of the three models considered above to win broad support amongst the political class because it does not establish a new legal structure in the Constitution. Rather it establishes a requirement to consult. This is not to say that the other two more detailed models of Twomey 2015 and Anderson, Davis, Pearson *et al* 2018 are flawed. They are both credible drafting attempts which may well be constitutionally sound, and which may well have more Indigenous support than Twomey 2020. Each of the three models should be kept on the table until a detailed review has been concluded. Ultimately, the drafting of the constitutional amendment needs to ensure that the Constitution requires consultation with Indigenous people. Each of the three models achieves this important goal. It's just that one option is considerably more politically viable than the other two given political developments since 2017.

Constitutional versus statutory voice

The first question many will ask is how would the Voice be bedded down? Would it be in statute or in the Constitution? Much of the debate has centred on this question—especially because of the false narrative about the 'third chamber'. The Uluru Statement calls for a constitutional Voice—but it does not spell out in detail how this would work. All it says is: "We call for the establishment of a First Nations Voice enshrined in the Constitution." There have been at least three approaches to implementing this call:

1. Voice established in Constitution
   Legislation to provide detail for Voice established in Constitution
2. Constitutional obligation to hear Indigenous voices
   Voice established in legislation
3. No change to Constitution in the short term
   Voice established in legislation

Option 1—constitutionally entrenched body

The first option would involve provisions for a body to be set out in the Constitution. No one has seriously proposed a highly detailed model. This is how a 'third chamber' could be imagined. Perhaps this model would be similar to the framework used in Chapter III where the Constitution sets out the details of the High Court.[45]

This chapter of the Constitution sets out a very basic frame which requires legislation to provide the bulk of the machinery. Another constitutional creation is the Inter-State Commission which has a very basic framework set out in the Constitution—it has not been used since 1990. The Inter-State Commission was cited by Ken Wyatt in public statements as an example of a body which had no modern usage despite being in the Constitution.

An amendment for a detailed body that is set out in the Constitution has no chance of being passed at a referendum. The scare campaign writes itself: it would be said that it is a risk to parliamentary supremacy that would undermine the equality of Australian citizens and would imperil the constitutional system. The more detail; the more risk of defeat. And, in reality, the detail does not need to be in the Constitution.

Option 2—constitutional obligation to consult

Setting out an obligation to consult with Aboriginal and Torres Strait Islander people is a less ambitious but more realistic approach given the history of constitutional reform in Australia. The Twomey 2020 model is a response to the rejection of the Twomey 2015 model as a 'third chamber'. It delivers a constitutional guarantee that Indigenous peoples will be heard on the laws which affect them. It then leaves the structure and the process for the federal parliament to assemble. This model has been further developed by Kerry Pinkstone, a visiting fellow at Australian Catholic University's public policy think-tank, the PM Glynn Institute, which released a paper in 2020 called *Anchoring our Commitment in the Constitution*. Pinkstone argues that "we can uphold the Constitution and the liberal values which underpin it and at the same time recognise Indigenous Australians within this very practical document."

This would, as Aboriginal leader and political activist, Warren Mundine said, look beyond symbolism to Indigenous aspirations for constitutional recognition on the one hand, and mainstream concerns about it on the other. I believe that this is the best model in keeping with the character of the Constitution whilst meeting the goals of the Indigenous people. It would, as Pinkstone argues, be a contribution to nation-building. The political risks of this approach are minimal. The practical operation of the Constitution has road-tested constitutional requirements for the Commonwealth to do certain things.

Former Chief Justice Murray Gleeson, appointed by John Howard, gave a speech that suggests this kind of approach keeps faith with the founding fathers' drafting framework: "A proposal that the Constitution should provide for Parliament to design, establish, and determine from time to time the make-up and operations of a body to represent Indigenous people, with a specific function of advising about the exercise of that power, hardly seems revolutionary." The legal soundness of this approach is not in doubt. Gleeson said in 2019 that

> the structure, composition and functions of the proposed representative body would be determined, and susceptible to change, by legislation of the Federal Parliament. What would appear in the Constitution would be the minimum requirements necessary to guarantee its continued existence and its essential characteristics.

It leaves the parliament in the driver's seat—as it should be under our system of parliamentary supremacy. The Commonwealth is constitutionally required to consult, but the parliament determines the legal framework for this consultation. The structure of the Voice could then be established in legislation by drawing upon the advice of the co-design work led by Marcia Langton and Tom Calma. There would be local and national voices to satisfy the constitutional obligation. This is the model the nation should adopt.

Option 3—legislation only

A legislated voice would be a government-established body, most likely a statutory authority, which would provide the Voice mechanism without a constitutional guarantee. In this scenario, the Voice would be legislated based on the advice of the Langton-Calma co-design process. There are many examples of different tiers of government using consultative bodies to engage Indigenous citizens. While this may be an effective mechanism, it does not have the constitutional guarantee for which the Uluru Statement calls.

The way forward

The Uluru Statement calls for constitutional reform. The Voice emerged from a discussion kicked off by John Howard on constitutional recognition. It should therefore end with a constitutional amendment. Ideally, a constitutional amendment and accompanying legislation to enact the Voice would be announced and delivered simultaneously. Yet that is not how the system of constitutional amendment works. Noel Pearson set out his preference for such a process in March 2021 at the National Museum:

> Let us complete the legislative design of the Voice, and produce an

exposure draft of the Bill so that all parliamentarians and the members of the Australian public can see exactly what the Voice entails. Let us set the Bill aside and settle on the words of constitutional amendment that recognises Indigenous Australians and upholds the Constitution, and put the amendment to a referendum of the Australian people at the next best opportunity.

While this would be an ideal scenario, the Voice reforms may need to be implemented over time because of the constraints of constitutional reform. It may not be possible to land the whole thing in one go. It may well be the case that the only way to get a Voice up and running—and guaranteed in the Constitution—is through a gradual approach. The timetable could be as short as just one parliamentary term, but we must be clear on what we are seeking to achieve and what is going where. Ambiguity is inappropriate and it may also kill any prospect for constitutional reform. There has been no successful constitutional amendment for almost fifty years. There will be great resistance to change, and the supporters of a Voice which is backed through a constitutional guarantee should be clear-eyed about avoiding ambiguity. Such ambiguity can be caused by legal uncertainty, but even if legal experts agree about the proposal, political obstacles can still confuse the debate and so an unambiguous proposal needs to avoid such political obstacles. As Marcia Langton says, "People need to know what they would be voting on. We would have to have a detailed answer."[46]

The way forward is to deliver a package that comprises a commitment to holding a referendum on a Voice and to legislating for a Voice—with legislation a possibility within the current parliament. The commitment to a referendum would be for the next parliamentary term, due to commence in 2022, probably on the Twomey 2020 model. This would provide the constitutional guarantee that ensures Indigenous voices are heard. The nation has spent almost two decades talking about constitutional recognition. The Indigenous community is clear that only substantive constitutional amendments will be acceptable. The best way to keep faith with Howard's 2007 commitment and the 2017 Uluru Statement, is to legislate a Voice and make the Twomey 2020 model our plan for constitutional recognition. This leaves the parliament in the driver's seat without limiting any legal capacity but guarantees Indigenous voices will be heard.

Treaty

As a supporter of the Uluru Statement, I find this element the most elusive of its three components. It means different things to different people. While there are strong views on the concept of a treaty, there is no consensus on what a treaty would mean or do. The Uluru Statement doesn't contain the word treaty. Rather it refers to "agreement making", by which it means agreements between governments and Indigenous peoples. There has already been some progress on this front. For example, the South West (Noongar) Land Agreement in Western Australia is a land and financial agreement between the Noongar people and the State of Western Australia.

In the past few decades, elements of a treaty have been delivered. The High Court of Australia overturned the concept of *terra nullius*—establishing native title, which was subsequently put on a statutory footing by the federal parliament. Australian parliaments have also legislated for Indigenous land rights, and such legislation has given large tracts of land to traditional owners. These are not treaties but they do address key elements of treaties: land and resources. The land rights schemes in the States are highly varied. Tim Rowse writes that "in the last third of the 20th century, nearly one fifth of the Australian land mass was transferred to Indigenous Australians' ownership. By 2013, Indigenous interests had been recognised over half of Australia—a combination of land rights, native title and Indigenous Land Use Agreements enabled by the assertion of native title."[47]

The parliament continues to consider the type of representation which ought to be afforded to Indigenous Australians (as set out above in the section on Voice). It is true that Australia does not have a formal treaty. But overseas attempts at domestic treaty processes are generally focused on the parliamentary or congressional processes and land rights. New Zealand's Treaty of Waitangi led to settlements—both land and financial. The United States's treaties with the Cherokee and Choctaw nations have entitled the latter to have an advisory vote in the United States Congress—a right that has been used sparingly. Equally, Canada's treaties have led to land claims—such as in the creation of the Province of Nunavut.

According to two constitutional experts, George Williams and Harry Hobbs, a treaty with an Indigenous people typically has three elements:

> First, recognition that Indigenous peoples are polities, and so are distinctive and differentiated from other citizens within the State. Second, that settlement is achieved via a broad-ranging political agreement . . . Third, that the State recognises or establishes, and resources, structures of culturally appropriate governance with powers of decision-making and control that amount to (at least) a limited form of self-government.[48]

In other words, a combination of land rights, native title, and a Voice.

It is also true that we are not someone else's colony: we are not an outpost of someone else's empire. We are one people of many different backgrounds. I say this as a first generation Australian, born to a British migrant. As Stan Grant says:

> I am an Australian. That is all I can be. I am a convict in irons on a ship called *Providence* . . . I am [a survivor] of the disease and violence that ravaged the first people of this land. I am John Grant and I am Frank Foster. I am the view from the ship and the view from the shore.

We are all Australian which makes a conventional 'treaty' very challenging and probably unworkable. The Commonwealth of Australia is sovereign at international law and it cannot enter into a treaty with itself—or with a part of itself.

Land rights and management of land is of special importance. This system is important because it can—and must—deliver economic advancement. As Alice Springs councillor Jacinta Price sums up the current problem, "In the Northern Territory, land councils are huge, they are basically redundant but are very powerful. They don't drive economic empowerment and there will never be progress while they are there." We should review our land rights regimes, including the land council system, to ensure they are driving economic development and self-determination.

Ultimately, the matters that make up the concept of a treaty, such as land and resources, need to be resolved at the local level between State governments and Indigenous nations, as the State of Western Australian Government and the Noongar peoples have done under a Liberal government. A national treaty would be of little practical value to the Noongar peoples, as the Commonwealth has little purchase in the matters which would meaningfully comprise a treaty. The idea of modern Australia negotiating with a 'sovereign' national Aboriginal body is unrealistic. Sovereignty is a post-Westphalian European concept which provides legal authority to a sovereign (be it royalty or an appointed or elected assembly). It is based on the idea of national states and has limited relevance to Aboriginal society, which is not and never was organized on the basis of having this form of legal 'sovereignty'.

However, the Uluru Statement speaks to 'spiritual' sovereignty which is compatible with the sovereignty of the Crown. The Crown is sovereign in the Westphalian sense, but the Indigenous peoples are sovereign in another sense. There could be different senses of sovereignty that are compatible with one another. When the Uluru Statement speaks of a spiritual notion of sovereignty, it is drawing on the idea in the International Court of Justice's *Advisory Opinion on Western Sahara*. The idea of spiritual sovereignty does capture what matters to Indigenous people about their connection to country, and this is something that endures—their connection to country endures and so too does their spiritual sovereignty.

Early treaty claims

In the early decades of the twentieth century, numerous petitions and claims were made, perhaps most notably by the Australian Aboriginals League and Aboriginal activist and community leader, William Cooper. Petitions and letters to prime ministers were set out, including by reconciliation campaigner, Pastor Sir Doug Nicholls, of the Yorta Yorta in the Murray-Goulburn region, who, in 1949, wrote to the prime minister, Ben Chifley, to ask for "support on behalf of my fellow members of the Australian Aboriginal race for our request that we be accorded representation in the Australian National Parliament."[49] Nicholls eloquently set out his stance: "the request is simply that, in order to provide an opportunity for a spokesman for my people in the National Parliament on their own native land." Some requests were for a Voice, like Nicholls's petition. Others sought land and reparations.

The Bark Petitions were another important marker in the history of Indigenous advocacy. In 1963, the Yolngu people petitioned the parliament. They sought reform to address the way their land was taken from them, explaining: "the procedures of the excision of this land and the fate of the people on it were never explained to them beforehand, and were kept secret from them."[50] The Bark Petitions did not yield change. Petitions and letters requesting substantial reform were not actioned and issues of representation were raised throughout the first sixty years of the federation. The wheels began to turn in the 1960s.

Modern treaty requests

Three proposals have been put forward in the past half century. The first of which was developed by the National Aboriginal Conference in 1979. It argued there should be a *makarrata* (Yolngu word) or treaty. This became the policy of the Fraser government. In 1979, the Conference issued a statement saying that "Aboriginal people are entitled to compensation for the loss of land. Aboriginals want recognition of their right to establish and to control their own organizations and run their own affairs." Fred Chaney, the minister at the time, responded, saying, "The Government welcomes this approach toward 'Makarrata'."[51] Instead, the Fraser government commissioned an inquiry into the concept of makarrata in 1981.

The National Aboriginal Conference's submission to the inquiry said that Aboriginal and Torres Strait Islander people had kept their sovereignty and nationhood and should be treated as equal in political status with the Commonwealth if a makarrata were to be pursued. Their submission said, "We are aware of Australian ambition to be one nation, one people. However, this cannot be achieved if our people are denied justice in accordance with international opinion relating to a people's right of self-determination . . ." The report of the Labor-chaired inquiry rejected the word 'treaty' due to the lack of international standing of Australia's Indigenous peoples.

The makarrata report was not tabled before the 1983 election. By that time, land rights had been delivered (in 1976), although their implementation took some time. For example, Uluru wasn't handed back to the traditional owners, the Anangu people, until 1985. What the makarrata inquiry did recommend was a new section in the Commonwealth Constitution (105B), which would allow the national government to establish a 'compact' between the government and Indigenous people. The Hawke government had a policy of a 'treaty', which followed the Barunga Statement's formal request for a treaty, although this was never delivered. The era of native title and further land rights occurred in the 1990s and the focus for the decade between 2007 and 2017 was on formulating symbolic constitutional recognition. While the notion of agreement making or treaty was put back on the table in the 2017 Uluru Statement, the land rights and native title regimes represent progress on the key elements of a treaty.

What does Uluru say?

It doesn't say treaty, but this word has been widely used in the marketing of the statement. Like each of the components of the statement, the detail for the big ideas is missing, leaving scope for development. It says:

> Makarrata is the culmination of our agenda: *the coming together after a struggle*. It captures our aspirations for a fair and truthful relationship with the people of Australia and a better future for our children based on justice and self-determination. We seek a Makarrata Commission to supervise a process of agreement-making between governments and First Nations and truth-telling about our history.

This section of the statement covers both treaty or agreement-making through a Makarrata Commission and truth-telling. Truth-telling is a more straightforward initiative for the Commonwealth to fund and help communities facilitate. But a treaty, as it may be popularly understood, is very difficult for Canberra to deliver on for two reasons: the States have the land and Australia is not someone else's colony.

States have the land

First, State governments are in the driver's seat because they control the land under our system of government. Treaties with Indigenous people are generally about land. From 1788, the parts of the Australian continent claimed by Arthur Philip for the King of the United Kingdom of Great Britain were held as Crown land under the colony of New South Wales. In time, there were additional colonies which held the land as Crown land and each colony was administered from a colonial capital city by its local legislature. The colonies of Australia held all the public land of Australia that wasn't secured as private tenure until the people of the colonies voted to establish a central government in the late nineteenth century. The non-Indigenous people of the colonies voted in favour of the proposed Commonwealth Constitution. The Constitution set out the powers of the central government and the constituent States (former colonies).

The creation of the Commonwealth in 1901 meant there would be a national government which had limited power apart from lands. On power, the Commonwealth would not have the power to legislate for people of the "Aboriginal race" for the first sixty-six years, until the Holt Government's successful referendum. It has only been for the past fifty years that the central government has been able to do anything of substantial importance on Indigenous matters. On land, the States retained ownership of Crown land, apart lands required for defence or for the operation of the Commonwealth government, and other territories acquired by the Commonwealth. According to Geoscience Australia:

> The Canberra-Yass district was chosen as the site of the new national capital in 1908. An area covering 2,358 square kilometres was ceded to the Commonwealth in 1911, forming the Australian Capital Territory. It was considered that the capital should have its own port and consequently the Jervis Bay Territory was formed in 1915 when land was surrendered to the Commonwealth by New South Wales.

The Australian Capital Territory is a very small part of the Australian landmass. A larger landmass in the control of the Commonwealth is the Northern Territory, which was the first jurisdiction to have land rights established by the Fraser Government in 1976. The territories remain outliers. The central government can only pass laws to regulate land of the territories but not for the bulk of the Australian landmass which is under control of the Australian states.

Ken Wyatt said in 2019:

> With respect to treaty, it's important that State and Territory jurisdictions take the lead. When you consider the Constitution, they are better placed to undertake that work. The West Australian land agreement by the Barnett Government is a treaty in the true sense. Treaty models are evolving with work undertaken by the Victorian and Northern Territory governments which address the aspirations of Indigenous Australians in those jurisdictions, and it's important that it resides and sits there.

The States' efforts on agreement-making is, therefore, most important. However, agreements which embody land rights must involve more than just handing over large tracts of land without an economic development plan. Regrettably, this is the situation I have witnessed in New South Wales. Land councils in the west of the State own the land but they have no real prospects for developing the country. This is perhaps most acute in New South Wales, where limited prospects for mining or other activities exist. Yolngu leader Galarrwuy Yunupingu says the land rights journey started out as a promising reform after Fraser passed his laws:

> All over the place Yolngu were moving back to their homelands, and there was good support and recognition for this work. I know because I was there. The homeland movement was proving very effective at bringing hope to people on the ground. Homelands were being set up everywhere: the Dhalwangu clan took back Gan Gan for us, as well as the homeland of Gurrumurru further north.[52]

Yunupingu says the introduction of self-government for the Northern Territory and welfare programmes undermined the land rights system. He says we have a long way to go to deliver reconciliation and that self-determination and self-management is key to reconciliation.

The States

There is insufficient space to consider the land rights laws in each Australian State in detail. Some of the clearer outcomes have been achieved in Western Australia and Queensland. The Western Australian South West Native Title Settlement (Noongar Settlement) is the largest native title deal in our history. It covers 30,000 people and 200,000 square kilometres. The Noongar Settlement includes recognition in an Act of the Parliament of Western Australia of the Noongar peoples' traditional ownership of the southwest. The total value of the settlement has been estimated to be $1.3 billion. It establishes a trust fund and organization for the Noongar people, with eventual capitalisation of $600 million. It sets up joint management of national parks and transfers of title (freehold or leasehold) of 320,000 hectares of land to the Noongar trust.

Constitutional lawyers George Williams and Harry Hobbs describe the Noongar agreement thus:

> By its very nature, the Noongar agreement is in fact a classic treaty; it is a coming together between two nations to agree upon certain things, and in doing so, finding a way forward together and recognising each other's sovereignty. By recognising each other's sovereignty, they decided how they would continue to coexist in a manner that they agreed to through negotiation. Yothu Yindi sung 'treaty now', and that is what we are doing here; this is a treaty between the government of Western Australia representing the newcomers, and the nation of the Noongar people.[53]

The Noongar peoples have described the agreement as "a great opportunity for our Noongar people to come together, to control our own destiny, and to build a solid future for generations to come."[54] I don't entirely agree with the characterization of "two nations" coming together to agree on certain things, but it is a comprehensive model for other Australian States to follow. The West Australian premier who delivered this agreement, Colin Barnett, said in 2015 that "this is an extraordinary act of self-determination by Aboriginal people and provides them with a real opportunity for independence." Barnett explains:

> Native title had been a disappointment and where there was mining in the north, the mining money was provided to a small group of people. Neither system was delivering for the people. They wanted economic independence which I backed in and I gave Glen Kelly [Noongar representative] hero status. He drew it together.

Another example is Queensland's *Aboriginal Land Act 1991* and *Torres Strait Islander Land Act 1991* which provided ownership of land to land trusts and corporations but also set up a land tribunal. The Hopevale land claim of 2011 saw freehold title over 110,000 hectares of land granted to the Hopevale Congress Aboriginal Corporation. It came with a payment of $6,500,000 to provide compensation for nearby mining. These schemes vary widely throughout the Australian States and are complemented by the Commonwealth's *Native Title Act 1993*.

Other issues which have been flagged by some groups, such as the incorporation of tribal law or different justice systems, also come under the purview of the States. But the substantive point is that the States have the land and, therefore, the negotiations about land rights, which are central to calls for a treaty, can only be delivered by the States. There are many other approaches across the Australian States. They differ greatly. An inquiry into the various systems and approaches to land rights should be conducted to promote economic development and sustainable self-determination.

In most cases, the land has been handed to land councils which have become powerful organizations. There are mixed views on whether this system has delivered the type of economic development which is desired. To whom do the economic gains accrue to under this system? Deceased Noongar leader Ken Colbung said in 1988 that "I am against turning land rights into material gain by a few."[55] It is paramount that these systems deliver for the whole Indigenous community and that we consider how the land rights system works alongside the natural desire for private property ownership amongst the burgeoning middle classes. A review of these arrangements should be conducted.

Australia is not someone else's colony

Secondly, the idea of a nineteenth-century-style treaty between an Indigenous people and a colonial power, is no longer relevant. It has been superseded by the passage of time and by the increasing success of Indigenous people. Australia is not someone else's colony. Australia has been its own country since 1901, the *Statute of Westminster 1931* marked the retreat of British intervention in Australian affairs, and the process of legal independence was completed with the passage of the *Australia Acts 1986*.

Further, Indigenous people have been successful in getting into almost every institution in our system of government. That means that a traditional treaty could not be negotiated between the 'government' and Indigenous people because Indigenous people are part of the government. At the time of writing, there are six Indigenous people in the national parliament, including one in the cabinet. They constitute 2.6% of the 227 Commonwealth parliamentarians, which is close to the 3% of Australians who are Indigenous. When the proposal for a treaty was developed in 1979, Neville Bonner was the only Indigenous person member of the federal parliament. Then, in 1988, when the Barunga Statement was presented to Bob Hawke, there were no Indigenous members of federal parliament.

Aiden Ridgeway, who belongs to the Gumbaynggirr people of the mid-north coast of New South Wales, would be the next Indigenous person to serve in the Senate between 1999 and 2005. Fast forward to the 2017 Uluru Statement and there were five serving Indigenous members, including Ken Wyatt who was serving as a minister. The significant improvement in numbers over the past forty-one years shows Indigenous people have become legislators and can increasingly set the terms of Australian governments themselves. That is the essence of a liberal democracy. We need to increase this proportion because it is a very important perspective to have inside the parliament—and it's important that Indigenous perspectives are heard inside all parties. Indigenous people don't have homogeneous political views—no group in Australian society does. The Liberal Party has delivered the bulk of the firsts—first Indigenous member, first cabinet minister, first Aboriginal Minister for Indigenous Australians. But we must have more Indigenous people inside our party. How we can achieve this is discussed below.

There could be an Indigenous prime minister in my generation of leaders. It would be a backward step for Australians to think of ourselves as a foreign people or that people who are born in our country but are not Aboriginal or Torres Strait Islander are somehow not native to Australia. Where would I go if I was not in Australia?

I am Australian. On the maternal side of my family, my children are the fourth generation born in this country. I don't think they will have an affinity with their forebears in the United Kingdom or in Ireland. That is what a treaty in the traditional Westphalian 'international relations' sense implies. I can only see the pursuit of a treaty, as popularly understood, getting harder over time.

The future

Indigenous Australians are breaking new ground all the time. As Stan Grant observes, an Indigenous middle class has developed in the past decade:

> Between 1996 and 2006, Aboriginal Australia was transformed. The number of educated, well-paid black professionals increased by 75 per cent. Take medicine as an example: the number of Indigenous GPs doubled from 41 to 82. The number of registered nurses jumped by 71 per cent.[56]

People from middle-class backgrounds tend to dominate the political establishment, so more middle-class Indigenous people means more Indigenous members of federal parliament. On the ground, this means people like Injarra Harbour. A descendent of the Koa people from Winton in central west Queensland, Harbour is the first Indigenous school captain at Brisbane's St Joseph's Nudgee College, and explains:

> My grandparents were forced to work on stations since they were ten years old and never got the opportunity to attend school so I am so grateful they stressed the importance of getting an education; and my parents too reinforced and really lived out the educational journey with me because I think they really recognise education as a tool to break down the barriers forced on Indigenous people.

Personally, I hope that more Indigenous Australians choose to engage in public service—one option is to serve in parliament. Under our system, even if we deliver the best Voice imaginable, the parliament will remain the supreme decision-making forum in Australia. More Indigenous parliamentarians will improve the diversity and strength of Canberra's policy perspective. They will also diminish the practical imperative for a treaty. Although it remains the aspiration of many Indigenous people, a treaty has become an unrealistic approach compared to the agreement-making envisioned in the Uluru Statement. Langton says:

> You have all these moving parts already [laws]. You have the [Victorian] Settlement Act, native title, Cultural Heritage Act and so on. I don't think there will ever be a national treaty. How could you bring together the extraordinary detail for it to make any sense? You can't. That's why we raised constitutional recognition.[57]

Truth

On truth, the Uluru Statement says: "We seek a Makarrata Commission to supervise . . . truth-telling about our history." Stan Grant sets out the strongest possible case for this idea. He says:

> Each Anzac Day Australians take the solemn pledge to always remember. There is something sacred about that oath; it has become a secular liturgy. Yet the irony is not lost on Indigenous Australians, that as a nation we still find it so easy to forget the worst of our history—the massacres, the disease, segregation and discrimination.

The Uluru Statement seeks the truth to be told through a national framework. This is a good idea if it is connected to the local histories as much as it reflects the national story of Australia. The word 'truth' is fine, but it bears connotations that we are not telling the truth now. Early on in my lifetime, I was educated with historian Henry Reynolds, and later, as an adult, I learned about

Stanner's Great Australian Silence. The truth *is* told in Australia. Can we do a better job? Yes, but the idea that we are all lying or denying the truth is no longer credible. It is important that we continue to look at the various historical perspectives. Our history isn't going anywhere. Perkins's edict, "We cannot live in the past, but the past lives in us," will always be true. This timeless line has been built upon by his daughter, Rachel Perkins, who said in her 2019 Boyer Lectures that "the past has made us. We are its inheritors, for better or worse and this is now our time." Brooke Boney reminds us that "truth-telling is the most important thing." She says, "So many of the issues are tied up in history."[58]

The question is what would a truth-telling framework do? Would it deliver a different syllabus in schools? Would it underwrite a public works programme to build statues and monuments to Indigenous leaders? This is where a Makarrata Commission or similar agency could do some good work. It could help facilitate local truth-telling, help with identifying traditional place names and with the repatriation of human remains, for instance. It could, if fairly constituted, provide an independent third party between the government and Indigenous people as seen in New Zealand.

The good and bad

Australia has a history which has been good and bad—we should be honest about it. As canvassed above, the history wars forced people, including the prime minister to the barricades in the 1990s and first decade of the twenty-first century. Much ink was spilt, and it is hard to tell how much was achieved during the history wars era. The barometer on history has swung to a position which better reflects the past, but we have more work to do. A 2016 book on Australian history published by one of the key warriors of the 1990s, Geoffrey Blainey, includes chapters called "Skeletons in the nation's cupboard" and "Wide spaces and deep silences". The good and the bad remains the best way to look at it. Because it is the truth.

The good, as David Kemp sets out in his five-volume series, *Australian Liberalism,* is very good. Australia led the world in developing a fast-moving liberal democracy which, for example, gave women the vote and the right to stand for election before almost every other nation. Australia has been a stable democracy which has settled millions of people since the Second World War. But Australia was built upon the active exclusion of Indigenous people from land and civic life. There is no question that the historical dispossession underwrote the success of modern Australia. Alistair Ferguson, an Indigenous man I met in central West Burke, told me:

> The arrival of 'first boat people' in 1788 in Australia and the colonisation of Australia by the British led to a structural process of disintegration of the Indigenous Nations. The colonists did not recognise the existence of the sixty-millennia-old Indigenous nations, identity, culture, heritage, and languages. Instead they regarded the continent as *terra nullius*—meaning "nobody's land". As a result, the process of structural dismantling of Indigenous nations and First Nation peoples was set in motion which led to the historic dispossession, injustice, creation of 'stolen generation' and intergenerational trauma and the marginalisation of the ATSI peoples in their own country.

This is the perspective which has been presented more widely in the past few decades.

The frontier

The better-balanced version of Australian history, as taught in schools, has been a big step forward. But it still feels that the frontier wars are not known as well as other Australian conflicts. David Kemp is an icon of liberalism. There is rigour to his philosophical frame but also balance. The early years of British settlement were tough. Kemp draws on estimates of the population falling from 750,000 in 1788 down to just 110,000 by 1901.[59] He argues that "the governments of the colonies had attempted, ineffectually, to protect Aboriginal people against the settlers' violence . . . the number of massacres involving five or more Aboriginal people during the colonial period has so far identified 200 such attacks in eastern Australia."[60]

Reynolds wrote in 1984 that "Aboriginal resistance emerged as one of the major problems of colonial society . . . [it was] surprisingly prolonged and effective, exacting a high price from many pioneer communities in tension and insecurity . . ." Reynolds estimates that 2,000 settlers and 20,000 Aboriginal people died on the violent frontier. Another historian, Jonathan Richards, estimates 20,000 Aboriginal people were killed in the process of colonisation in Queensland alone, where "there is much more money spent on killing Aboriginal people than there is feeding them." The massacres were real. Of that there is no question. Only the numbers are uncertain. The question is how does this fit into our history as a nation today.

Settlement versus invasion

Was Australia *settled* or was it *invaded*? The truth is both. It was certainly not *discovered*. Even Cook's secret instructions from the British Admiralty recognised this point:

> You are also with the consent of the Natives to take Possession

of convenient Situations in the Country, in the Name of the King of Great Britain; Or, if you find the Country uninhabited, take Possession for His Majesty by setting up proper Marks & Inscriptions, as first Discoverers & Possessors.

During the late eighteenth century, the world was getting smaller. European ships were breaking new ground and planting their flags in foreign lands. It was inevitable that there would be meetings as occurred at Botany Bay in 1770 and later in the interior. The Spanish, Portuguese, and Dutch had been here and the French were closing in.

Stan Grant writes that "the story of Australia begins on that shore, when a people of steam and steel met a people of flint and bone and wood. A people of Enlightenment met a people of the Dreaming. They danced, briefly on that shore . . . Soon the frontier wars would ignite: years of killing would begin. Between the dance and destruction is the Australian dream."[61] The taking of a land by force would be an invasion in a war environment. In many parts of the country, that's what it was. It was an occupation, but one where the same legal system ultimately handed back more than half the continent to the successors of those alive in the eighteenth century. The land was taken. Stan Grant explains, "I was born into poverty because our inheritance was taken. The wealth of Australia is based on land taken." The internal conflicts of Australia have now been well profiled as civil, not military history.

The military history of Australia focuses on armed conflict where the Anzacs have performed heroic deeds to help liberate Europeans and our own people from the forces of evil. I am proud of our contribution to the security of the world. Australia made a disproportionate contribution to the war efforts in the First and Second World Wars. My own family was represented in the

Second World War through my only Australian-born grandparent, James Paton. He served our country in the Middle East and the Pacific, where there was active discrimination against Indigenous servicemen who served with him. Noel Pearson said in 1997 of these two worlds:

> It is a troubling business coming to terms with Australian history, both for Aboriginal people and non-Aboriginal people. For our people, it is a troubling business because there is the imperative of never allowing anyone to forget the truths of the past but to be able as a community to rise above its demoralising legacy . . . it's also a challenge for non-Aboriginal Australia, a challenge to understand that in the same way that they urge pride in Gallipoli and in Kokoda . . . can we as a community and a nation also acknowledge the shameful aspects of the past.

Pearson presents a truth that many Australians have never processed. Because they haven't needed to. There is a level of comfort in an incomplete history of Australia because it only presents the good, and not the bad. Comfortable. That is a word that comes up regularly. We are too comfortable with our history because we haven't been prepared to consider the full picture. Maybe it's a combination of things: we don't want to consider the full picture because part of it is ugly.

The other part is linked to the lack of proximity most Australians have to Indigenous people. The full picture of Australian history is not part of their lives. Dispossession has not impacted their lives. Galarrwuy Yunupingu recollects a fishing expedition with Malcolm Fraser when he was prime minister:

> I try to put words in his mind about the importance of land, about the importance of respect, about giving things back in a proper way, not a halfway thing. But the Prime Minister is preoccupied with catching barramundi—he's not listening; he doesn't have to.

Indeed, in Fraser's memoir, he refers to "a boatload of fish".[62] The truth will make us uncomfortable because some of it is bad. As Stan Grant says, "our foundation story is incomplete without also Bennelong, Pemulwuy, the Appin Massacre, the Wiradjuri wars." Pearson nominates other warriors: Yagan, Windradyne, and Jandamurra. These are the names of people involved in the most significant conflict on Australian land. We should remember them.

Schools and history

In 2014, I purchased and read Noel Pearson's quarterly essay: *A Rightful Place: Race, recognition and a more complete Commonwealth*. I know this because I generally write my name inside books with the date of purchase. And sometimes location! It is a form of diary-keeping for a busy and sometimes forgetful person.

The next generation is even more aware of the full presentation of Australian history—I have noticed it in my own children. They speak of Gadigal, they are very interested in Aboriginal culture and art—which after all, is part of their inheritance as Australians. The 2018 Dodson-Leeser Committee made a recommendation that

> the Australian Government support the process of truth-telling. This could include the involvement of local organizations and communities, libraries, historical societies and Aboriginal and Torres Strait Islander associations. Some national coordination may be required, not to determine outcomes but to provide incentive and vision. These projects should include both Aboriginal and Torres Strait Islander peoples and descendants of local settlers. This could be done either prior to or after the establishment of the local voice bodies.

Enlisting the local voice groups could be an elegant solution. Localising truth-telling within each community makes a good deal of sense, but what about the curriculum today? The Australian

Curriculum includes history from years 7-10. Ancient history contains a unit where there is study of Indigenous history and culture. Modern history looks at "movements for changes, the progress towards recognition and equality for Aboriginal and Torres Strait Islander people and the focus of continued efforts." In addition, there is a separate project to promote Indigenous content in the classroom. History is a core subject in the Australian Curriculum, which gives students the opportunity to understand the core history of our country. It occurred in my day and appears to be further embedded today. This is real progress. More could be done to ensure Indigenous people have their say and express their understanding of what happened. A Makarrata Commission or similar institution could help deliver local histories from multiple perspectives—this could complement what is taught in schools.

What does it look like on the ground?

Myall Creek in northern New South Wales provides an example of local community engagement in truth-telling and history. On 10-11 June 1838, John Henry Fleming led a party of eleven stockmen armed with pistols, fowling pieces, swords, and cutlasses, with which they massacred at least twenty-eight Wirryaraay people. The bodies were burnt the following day. Unlike preceding or subsequent massacres, eleven of the perpetrators were arrested and tried (twice) for their actions, with seven subsequently being hanged. The remaining four walked free after Yintayintin, an Aboriginal witness who was to give testimony, "disappeared under mysterious circumstances".[63] Fleming, who was from a wealthy squatter family, evaded justice and subsequently became a justice of the peace.

The trial did not succeed in preventing future massacres. Rather, it established a frontier 'code of silence', under which perpetrators swore each other to secrecy; bodies were thoroughly burned; and government reports employed euphemisms such as 'dispersal' to hide the actions of frontier police and settlers. At Myall Creek in 2000, a memorial was dedicated which has brought local community and school groups into the story over the last two decades. It serves as living history, living truth. The curator of the memorial, Ivan Roberts, explains:

> There are two Myall Creek stories. The dreadful massacre of 1838 perpetrated against our First Peoples, the truth of which has to be acknowledged and told. The second story is that of the Myall Creek Memorial dedicated in 2000. Both stories need to be told but it is our desire and belief that the second story will help shape a positive future for our First Peoples and all Australians together.[64]

Ken Wyatt identifies Myall Creek as a model for truth-telling. He observed in 2020 that "Aboriginal and non-Aboriginal people came together, acknowledged their past history of an event that left a deep scar." He said it should be replicated across our nation, as should the dual naming of towns and regions, and these would be a big step forward.

What does truth look like beyond education?

Beyond proper education which tells the full balance of our history, our relationship with the truth is also apparent in how we manage public spaces. A vision for Indigenous culture inside Canberra's Parliamentary Triangle was set out above. But the States also have an important role to play. In South Australia, the premier, Steven Marshall, is building a new $200 million Aboriginal Art and Cultures Centre in Adelaide which will be 15,000 square metres and bigger than the renowned Art Gallery and Museum combined.

In Victoria, a proposal was developed by the First People's Assembly to establish a truth commission. The Yoo-rrook Justice Commission was established in March 2021 by the Victorian Government to examine the impact of colonisation on Indigenous people. It is expected to examine the ongoing impact of massacres, displacement, and policies of discrimination. Yorta Yorta man Ian Hamm said, "The victors get to write history. That will be an important part of the truth-telling commission's role. It will be told from the Aboriginal perspective." By addressing the past, this concept could help current and future generations build upon the gains in the classroom if it is properly resourced and supported by Indigenous and community groups. But education remains the key. There is good and there is bad.

Uluru summary

Before summarising what I think we should do with Uluru, it is worth considering again the liberal and conservative orthodoxy of the Uluru Statement. The arguments on the liberal and conservative side of politics for doing something will generally differ from a centre-left perspective. That was the case with same-sex marriage. Paul Ritchie's conservative case for marriage presented arguments to strengthen the institution of marriage—certainly not an argument of the left. This summary starts with a hard truth. Years on from Uluru, few Australians know what it is. The reality is that many Indigenous people have no idea what Uluru is either. Yet within liberal and conservative quarters, there is hostility towards the Uluru Statement. There have been three main reasons these groups have not wanted to support it.

Three reasons to do nothing

First, many liberals and conservatives have ridden the wave of the Turnbull government's characterization of the Voice as a 'third chamber'. The Turnbull, Joyce, and Scullion positioning on Uluru set the course which has been followed by almost all others. Secondly, many conservatives in particular simply do not want to see any constitutional changes—symbolic or substantive. Thirdly, there is no real constituency for Indigenous people. Most Australians don't know an Indigenous person and the same extends to the political class. The fact that there are very few votes in these matters makes it harder as the pressure drops away.

What should be done?

What should we do with the Uluru Statement? The Voice is a good idea which should have been in place some time ago, in fact, it was in the form of the National Aboriginal Conference during the Fraser years and then the flawed Aboriginal and Torres Strait Islander Commission during the Hawke-Keating-Howard period. The Voice is clearly the most important component of the Uluru Statement.

The idea of a national treaty seems impractical and has been superseded by the desire for a Voice, constitutional recognition, native title, land rights, and truth-telling. Some people think the Native Title Act goes too far; others that it does not go far enough, but everyone agrees that the Commonwealth needs the legislative power to amend it one way or another.

Truth-telling is essential and something a new Makarrata Commission or the existing Australian Institute of Aboriginal and

Torres Strait Islander Studies could help coordinate across the nation. That is, two out of three components should be progressed: Voice and Truth should proceed. A review of land rights and native title to ensure they are working to drive economic development would be a good idea. 'Treaty' remains unclear and undefined.

Exploding the arguments against Uluru

There are four major arguments against action on Uluru:

1. It is divisive;
2. Race has no place;
3. Indigenous people are well compensated; and
4. It is risky to amend the Constitution.

It is divisive

It is inescapable that the desire to be part of the nation's birth certificate (the Constitution), shows the desire of Australia's First Peoples to be part of the modern Australian project. As a country without some formal recognition of Indigenous people in the Constitution (or equivalent), and without a formal agreement or treaty, the request to be embedded in our constitutional system can only reflect the desire to build Australia—not divide it.

As the Uluru Statement says, it aims to build Australia up: "With substantive constitutional change and structural reform, we believe this ancient sovereignty can shine through as a fuller expression of Australia's nationhood." Some of the Indigenous opponents of Uluru have asked why Indigenous Australians would want to be part of the 'white man's Constitution'. Happily, this appears to be a minority position.

But it might not be forever. In time, an agenda to establish a separate constitutional system could become a serious request. For now, too many of the hardened activists who want to 'abolish' Australia by throwing the Constitution into the sea are on the fringes and have dealt themselves out of the debate. There has been and will continue to be a full spectrum of ideas on addressing Indigenous disadvantage and historical grievances. Everything from abolish Australia to reserved seats in the federal parliament have been floated in recent years. One consequence of the skewed commentary on the Uluru Statement is that the misconceptions about Uluru have been amplified. Calling it a third chamber or black parliament means it has grievously misrepresented it.

Many Australians, perhaps the bulk, have misgivings about providing resources and special treatment to Indigenous people. They often ask, "Why are we deploying a policy or law just for Aboriginals?" The answer, of course, is because the Indigenous people are the only people who have had special laws made for them on a continuing basis since 1788. This will continue to be the case. The enduring ancient connection between Indigenous people and the land has been reaffirmed in a bipartisan manner in native title, land rights, and a range of other laws.

Australia will always need to maintain special laws to recognise an ongoing connection between the land and the Indigenous people. Providing a better mechanism to deal with these policies and laws, and embedding it in our Constitution, can only be a uniting project. We will all be subject to the same laws in our liberal democracy. Indigenous people will simply have a new mechanism on the additional laws which apply to them. This is uniting, not dividing.

Race has no place

Race has always had a place in Australia. This fact has been well and truly chronicled in this book. Groups like the Samuel Griffith Society of constitutional conservatives and the Institute of Public Affairs, a centre-right think-tank, argue that the Uluru Statement would further entrench race. The Institute of Public Affairs argued on 2 June 2017, after the Uluru Statement was published, that:

> Race has no place in the Australian constitution. Proposals to grant special legal rights to any group of Australians based on their race will be rejected. Australians are egalitarian. Fairness is a concept that runs deep in the Australian psyche . . . This is why—if we are to make any changes to the constitution—we should ensure that any references to race are removed, not added. Currently there are two sections of the constitution that refer to race. The first is section 25, which was designed to discourage state governments from banning people of any particular race from taking part in elections. The second is section 51 (xxvi), which grants the Commonwealth the power to pass race-based laws. If Australians are to be asked to change the constitution it is this change that should be supported— the deletion of the two provisions that make reference to race. But anything that seeks to insert race back into the constitution is dangerous and divisive.

The extension of this position is that we should repeal the existing races power (including the power won in 1967). That would result in the collapse of the native title regime, possibly land rights, heritage protection laws, and a range of other laws set up for the benefit of Indigenous people. There would be virtually no support for this amongst any political party in Australia. It will never happen. I have been a member of the Institute of Public Affairs for some time. I think that the organization does a fine job in laying the philosophical foundations for a free society and a strong market-based economy. But I do not agree with its Race

Has No Place campaign. It has no basis in fact and expresses an unrealistic position.

As I said in my First Speech to the Australian Senate:

> Further, the campaign that "race has no place" in the Constitution may sound good but it is a campaign that should have been run in the 1890s as we crossed that Rubicon in 1901. Yes, our present Constitution already contains race in several places. It has a history which has been both good and bad. Today, the races power provides the Constitutional authority for the Native Title Act. Although some would extend Native Title rights and others would wind them back, everyone agrees this Parliament should retain this authority and power.

We crossed the Rubicon on race 120 years ago when we prevented the Commonwealth from legislating with respect to Indigenous people or counting them in the census. The reality is that Indigenous people will maintain an ongoing distinctive place in our constitutional and legal system—the races power underpins more than two dozen Acts of federal parliament where we make special laws for Indigenous people. Too often the people arguing race has no place are the same people arguing against any integration of Indigenous culture into Australian civic life. For example, in a speech setting out his opposition to a Voice, former Treasury secretary John Stone said in 2017:

> I begin with a welcome to country—a welcome to our country . . .
> So let me begin by acknowledging the traditional owners of this
> land: King George III, and his heirs and assigns.

This is the type of stuff I would hear as a young adult, which for the most part, has not been a part of my generation's perspective on traditional custodianship. Whether we like it or not, race is part of our system. This is the widely held position in comparable nations—the United States, Canada, and New Zealand.

Indigenous people are well compensated

$33 billion is spent on programmes for Indigenous Australians each year. The Uluru reforms will not materially add to this significant sum of money. Plenty of people are rightly concerned about accountability and transparency over the expenditure of money in Aboriginal programmes. They concur with the Productivity Commission report challenging the effectiveness of the annual funding for Indigenous Affairs across health, education, and welfare.

The report was critical of accountability and called for a step-by-step guide for assessing whether money had been well spent. The community members I speak to agree, many of them told us to our faces they just don't know where the money is going. The Commission received 180 submissions and said many programmes were developed without adequate consultation with Aboriginal and Torres Strait Islander communities.

The Cape York Institute submission said: "Given that the total spend on Indigenous affairs in Australia is nearing $35 billion annually it seems perverse and a measure of the problems, that under the current 'system' monitoring and evaluation does not improve results." Productivity Commissioner Romlie Mokak, a Djugun Yawuru man from the Kimberley, who is the first Indigenous commissioner and a former chief executive of the Lowitja Institute, says the policies and programmes are just not working as well as needed; that many of the efforts to find out if they'd been effective were 'ad hoc' or afterthoughts:

> Evaluation can play an important role filling this gap but regrettably
> it is often an afterthought and of poor quality. Importantly,
> Aboriginal and Torres Strait Islander people are rarely asked about

what or how to evaluate, or what evaluation results mean.

Mokak is right when he says evaluation is about understanding what's working, what isn't working, and what changes need to be made to make policies and programs work better. There is no shortage of cash but there is a shortage of thought and consultation. While it is true that Indigenous people control more than half of the Australian land mass, they do not get a say over the laws which underpin native title.

It is risky to amend the Constitution

On face value, it is risky to amend the Constitution. Therefore, perhaps the most compelling argument against adopting Uluru is the view that it could undermine or in some way damage the Australian constitutional system. There are certainly models which could effectively become a third chamber. It would imperil the Constitution if there were a detailed body prescribed in the Constitution. This would be totally out of character with our practical but effective Constitution. It all depends on how the amendments are drafted. The model developed most recently by Anne Twomey (Twomey 2020) is the model which would provide a constitutional guarantee without risking the operation of the constitutional system. Twomey's 2015 drafting which is a more expansive amendment than her 2020 model has been supported by Murray Gleeson which provides assurance the system will not be imperiled.

As set out above, her model is simply that "The Commonwealth shall make provision for Aboriginal and Torres Strait Islander peoples to be heard by the Commonwealth regarding proposed laws and other matters with respect to Aboriginal and Torres Strait Islander affairs, and the Parliament may make laws to give effect to this provision." As Twomey explains:

> This approach, which is modelled on sections 119 and 120 of the Constitution, places the obligation in the right place. It is the Commonwealth of Australia—the nation as a whole—that is obliged to ensure Aboriginal and Torres Strait Islander peoples are heard in relation to their own affairs. But it leaves open the means of giving effect to that obligation—it could be by government action, legislation, a parliamentary committee, or a combination of all of them.

This is a proportionate approach which reflects the principles set out in my First Speech. It is also in keeping with the drafting of the Constitution, which has been a very successful charter of government. I too am a constitutional conservative and I have also been a member of the Samuel Griffith Society, which is committed to upholding the Constitution as prepared by the founding fathers. The founding fathers included section 128 which has provided for eight separate changes to the Constitution since 1901. The founding fathers drafted the Constitution so that it could be updated over time. The bones have proven to be sound but incremental changes have occurred—such as the 1967 referendum.

3

Burradja Tomorrow— the future

HAVING CONSIDERED PAST CONTRIBUTIONS and the present reforms (Closing the Gap) as well as the latest request for structural reforms (in the Uluru Statement), the remaining pages in this book are devoted to the future. I hope my views reflect my commitment to the approach of *doing with* rather than *doing to* on Indigenous policy, as well as my own spin on the ideas put forward by others. As a policymaker, listening to people, as well as being prepared to advance my own ideas, is an article of faith for me. This means more listening to Indigenous people from all walks of life. But it's important that non-Indigenous people have a place in these debates. Sometimes, this can be a difficult space. I generally try to bring honesty about my own background and my limited personal experience to the table as my way of engaging. I have generally found the response to be remarkably good.

As I have explained, the Uluru Statement is a pivotal contribution to nation-building. In the coming years, I hope to help deliver on the elements of Voice and truth-telling. There now exists a substantial body of work on how a Voice could operate and the institutions required to assist with truth-telling can easily be repurposed or established. But there is more we should do to complement the partnership set up by Scott Morrison on Closing the Gap and the improvement he has made to Advance Australia Fair. Wherever the country's political leadership lands on Uluru, it is important that we start with Closing the Gap and the Uluru Statement, because these are the policy solutions either negotiated or requested by Indigenous people. Here is what I think we should do with Uluru in summary:

- Voice

  - Legislate for a national Voice and local Voice based on the Langton-Calma co-design process;

  - Commit to hold a referendum in the 47th Parliament.

- Treaty

  - Conduct a national review of land rights and native title laws to ensure they are driving economic development;

  - Consider establishing an independent tribunal capable of conducting agreements between Indigenous people and governments, and this tribunal should also assist with geographical place names and the repatriation of human remains.

- Truth

  - Commission local Voice groups or AIATSIS to assist communities develop multiple historical perspectives.

As canvassed above, we should always be looking for ways to drive economic development within the Indigenous community because economic capacity is a heavy focus of the Closing the Gap framework. But we should also review the land rights and native title regimes to ensure they are driving economic growth. In many cases, the system probably does not work well. Often land rights regimes do not provide for property rights for individuals which has been a key feature of economic success within liberal systems. The review must assess whether property rights can be compatible with a collectivist land rights regime.

On symbolic matters, we should also adopt some changes by permanently displaying Indigenous flags inside Parliament House and creating a National Resting Place inside the Parliamentary Triangle.

In this chapter, I set out four additional proposals that we should pursue:

1. We should settle a Declaration of Recognition;

2. We need more Indigenous people in Parliament—especially in the Liberal Party;

3. We should establish an assessment framework for the Uluru reforms; and

4. We should set goals for 2067—the centenary of the 1967 referendum.

Declaration

We should establish a declaration of recognition outside the Constitution. The declaration of recognition should reflect the three layers of Australia as set out by Noel Pearson—an ancient Indigenous heritage, British institutions, and multicultural gift.

A fuller expression of Australia Day and what it means should appear on 26 January each year. To move the day would be to avoid telling the truth.

By the end of the 47th Parliament, a package of changes to deliver the Uluru agenda should be delivered to consolidate Australia. Tying in Indigenous heritage and recognition will strengthen our democracy and the nation as it provides the fullest expression of our country, its history, and its unique profile.

Three proposals should be considered:

1. An Australian declaration of recognition of Indigenous people known as the Australian National Declaration should be developed;

2. The Declaration would be issued on 27 January and this becomes a national public holiday known as Buraadja Day; and

3. Australia Day would be retained on 26 January and a national approach to help facilitate truth telling is to be established.

These are largely important symbolic changes, unlike the reforms sought through the Uluru process. Accordingly, the declaration should be tied into staggered delivery of the bulk of the Uluru Statement's priorities. In total, there would be a serious package of legal, constitutional, and symbolic changes to consolidate our country.

A declaration of recognition could set out in a formal way the Pearson formulation of the Indigenous heritage, British institutions, and multicultural gift. It would be part of consolidating the Australian project like few other ideas.

As a patriot, I have never bristled at embracing my country and I have often struggled to understand how others haven't also done so. My sense is the majority are with me. Accordingly, a declaration or any similar national statement must be unifying and reflective of the majority. I have long admired the development of this idea, initially by my good friend, Julian Leeser, and his collaborator, Damien Freeman. This dynamic duo put the declaration on the map. The beauty of the declaration is that it could be legislated by the federal parliament, issued to all Australians and could be achieved without the risks of radically altering the Constitution.

Why would we do this?

It would be a meaningful but deliverable declaration which would present the full picture of Australian nationhood. This could be done without imperiling the Constitution. It would obviate the need for a risky preamble which could give rise to varied or strange interpretations by the High Court. As Twomey notes, the High Court has regularly drawn upon the words in the preamble:

> Another common use of the preamble is as an expression of Australia's nationhood, because the agreement was to unite in 'one indissoluble Federal Commonwealth', rather than a conglomeration of States. The preamble has also been used as support for and against the conclusion that the basis of federation was 'popular', as the agreement to unite was made by the 'people' rather than the colonies.[1]

Further, Freeman and Leeser set out the dangers of putting poetry in the Constitution in their chapter in *The Forgotten People*. They cite former High Court Chief Justice Harry Gibbs who warns that preambles can be very dangerous. Gibbs explains that a preamble could "significantly affect ministers and other executive officers in the exercise of their discretionary powers . . . in addition there can be no doubt that reliance could be placed on the words of the preamble by interested groups . . ."[2] As the former United States Supreme Court Justice Antonin Scalia said, "If you want aspirations, you can read the Declaration of Independence," but "there is no such philosophising in our Constitution," which is "a practical and pragmatic charter of government."

The new Australian declaration approach provides a way to pick up the work of the various reports and committees which were delivered in the lost decade from 2007-2017. The Dodson/ Leibler 2012 Expert Panel report to Julia Gillard grappled with the question of recognition in detail. It recommended a new section 51A which would have established recognition inside the body of the Constitution. It would have set out four separate headings to "recognise", "acknowledge", "respect", and "advance" Indigenous people. This would be totally out of step with the tenor and legal approach of the Constitution. For good reason, it was not adopted. The 2012 report appears to be based on the need for a section inside the Constitution because symbolism in the preamble would not cut it with Indigenous people:

> A statement of recognition in a preamble without any change to the operative text of the constitution would be likely viewed by in particular Aboriginal and Torres Strait Islander people as an inadequate form of recognition.[3]

The problem is that this is not a legal argument and it does not take the option of a declaration outside the Constitution into account.

What would it say?

Stan Grant proposed that it say:

> The first people touched this land as our continent was being formed. They came in boats when humanity had yet to cross an open sea. Here they formed a civilisation that continues to this day.

Their birthright has never been ceded. Those people live still in their descendants. We enter into their heritage and respect their traditions.

We honour too those who have come from other lands and carry with them their cultures and faiths. Though our bonds may strain, we seek to live together in harmony.

Though we may disagree, we find no enemy among us. We cherish the foundations of our nations, and our rule of law and democracy. We abide by the will of the majority but defend the rights of the minority. We are all equal in dignity.

Opportunity is for all. Worth should be measured not in privilege. By our efforts we prosper. In a land of plenty, we care for those without. From the first footsteps, we form a new people bound not by the chains of history but committed to a future forged together.

John Howard's proposed new preamble in 1999 (which was defeated at a referendum) read:

With hope in God, the Commonwealth of Australia is constituted by the equal sovereignty of all its citizens.

The Australian nation is woven together of people from many ancestries and arrivals. Our vast island continent has helped to shape the destiny of our Commonwealth and the spirit of its people.

Since time immemorial our land has been inhabited by Aboriginals and Torres Strait Islanders, who are honoured for their ancient and continuing cultures.

In every generation immigrants have brought great enrichment to our nation's life.

Australians are free to be proud of their country and heritage, free to realise themselves as individuals, and free to pursue their hopes and ideals. We value excellence as well as fairness, independence as dearly as mateship.

Australia's democratic and federal system of government exists under law to preserve and protect all Australians in an equal dignity which may never be infringed by prejudice or fashion or ideology nor invoked against achievement.

In this spirit we, the Australian people, commit ourselves to this Constitution.

My 100-word effort would be:

Australia is our country. A land of rich, bountiful, and rare beauty.

The fusion of the Dreaming, the British institutions, and multiculturalism enriches us all.

We are one indissoluble Commonwealth which we the people voted to establish.

We love this country.

We pay our respects to the ancient culture just as we revere our liberal democratic institutions.

A fair go, freedom, and equality of opportunity are core to our being.

We are one but we are many. We tell the truth as we go forward together.

Our loyalty is pledged to Australia, our people, and our institutions. In unity. Together, we Advance Australia.

I am certain that someone with better prose and a more creative mind could come up with a better set of words!

What would the process be?

There could be a contest established by the Australia Day Council to design the words for the Australian National Declaration. The preferred words could be circulated for public consultation before the parliament settles on two preferred options. A plebiscite could then be held to agree which of the options would be adopted as the declaration.

What would be done with it?

The declaration would be issued on 27 January at a ceremony in Canberra. The words would be inscribed onto the face of the national resting place. It would be sent out to all schools and embedded into the curriculum. Once declared on Declaration Day, 27 January would become a public holiday known as Buraadja Day.

Australia Day

Australia Day is emblematic of the ongoing history wars. The most recent polls show most Australians believe that the day should remain where it is. A recent poll from the Institute of Public Affairs shows 82% of people are proud to be Australian and 69% believe Australia Day should be on 26 January. The majority of Australians are rightly proud of our country. Many of British origin feel that the modern development of Australia which commenced with the arrival of the First Fleet on 26 January 1788 is an occasion worthy of being marked. In this section, I set out the case to keep Australia Day on 26 January, how the day should change, and how to conclude the history wars.

Under these proposals, Australia Day would be the day for reflecting on the Australia of Yesterday and how it has contributed to the Australia of Today. Buraadja Day would be a day dedicated to the Australia of Tomorrow, and how the Australia of Today might give rise to our aspirations for the Australia of Tomorrow.

Keep Australia Day

As Charlie Perkins said, we don't live in the past but the past lives in us. We cannot change the day that modern Australia commenced. There are three main reasons to keep the date. First, we should be honest about this date—the good and the bad. We should present both sides of the story. A false choice is often presented. It would be a big mistake to pretend this date wasn't the day that the continent's future changed forever. To pretend that there was another day would be turning our back on truth telling.

Stan Grant says:

> Australia Day is more than a day, it is more than a date—whatever that date may be. Moving the date or abolishing Australia Day does not answer the question—who are we? I fear moving the date would only hand it to those who would reclaim it as a day of white pride, turning it into a bombastic day of division . . . The future Australia Day will still likely be a day or protest, a day of sadness and a day of joy and thanks. We are all of those things.

Secondly, the date will not yield any significant changes to people's lives. It rarely comes up when you seek community advice on the issues that really matter to people on the ground. The issues which come up are generally related to day-to-day issues upon which the Voice can help. I have found that there is generally a very strong level of affinity for the Aboriginal flag throughout the community. The loss of the use of the flag within some communities has caused consternation.

Thirdly, moving the date will never satisfy the hardcore Abolish Australia activists. Accordingly, whilst I accept many people have legitimate reasons to seek a new date, many are advocating it as part of a shallow campaign.

Fourthly, it denies the incredible resilience of the Indigenous people. Linda Burney has said:

> January 26 is a reminder, not only of the dispossession and injustice, but also our strength and survival as a people and as a culture . . .

214

By all means, celebrate Australia Day, but let's use it as a day of reflection as well.

A similar theme is echoed by Ken Wyatt: "It's right to say that Indigenous Australians are survivors. Not only are we survivors, but we contribute much to the success of our great nation."

This sentiment was captured in a new campaign in 2020 through the Australia Day Council which focused on keeping the day and making it better. The campaign is called We're All Part of the Story. The minister responsible for Australia Day, Ben Morton, said, "Australia Day has in the past been too much about celebrating and not enough about reflecting and respect . . . it is also a day where we respectfully learn about the history, traditions, and cultures of Aboriginal and Torres Strait Islander peoples whose way of life was more than disrupted but has made possible what Australia is today."

Change the date

The date of Australia Day moved during the twentieth century. Australia Day was settled in 1994 as the national day. Aboriginal civil rights activist Jack Patten, who lived on the Cummeragunja Reserve on the border between New South Wales and Victoria, said on the first day of mourning on 26 January 1938, "On this day the white people are rejoicing. But we, as Aboriginals, have no reason to rejoice on Australia's 150th birthday." Reconciliation Australia says:

National days the world over are generally considered as occasions of celebration. In Australia, our national day is promoted as a time to reflect on the nation's achievements and what makes us proud to be Australian. Many Aboriginal and Torres Strait Islander Australians

wish to celebrate the values and freedoms that Australians enjoy but
do not feel that 26 January is an appropriate date to do so.

But changing the day will not change anything substantive. The clock will not wind back for those who want it to do so. While the Abolish Australia Day activists seem to assemble a large group each January, they are not representing the mainstream Indigenous feeling, and certainly not the mainstream non-Indigenous view. It is more likely that Abolish Australia Day is code for Abolish Australia. Keeping the day provides a fine entree into truth-telling. A nationally facilitated programme of truth-telling can be built into the national life as set out in part two. To change the day would only undermine truth-telling.

Indigenous members

We need more people in the parliament who bring the perspective of Indigenous Australia—I am especially keen that we do this in the Liberal Party. The Liberal Party should adopt a target of Indigenous people constituting 3% of its federal party room. Similar targets should be adopted by other parties too. If Labor and the Greens did the same, it would double the number of Indigenous parliamentarians. This is the best way to hear Indigenous voices on all policy matters—and would be far better than going for reserved seats in the Senate or House of Representatives, which would be most illiberal.

We need more Indigenous members of parliament—this is to complement the Uluru reforms. The perspective that Ken Wyatt has brought into the Liberal Party is highly valued. It is a perspective we must maintain permanently. Jacinta Price says, "When you come across an Aboriginal conservative, hold onto them because they're worth their weight in gold."

If parliament seems to lack diversity, it is mainly because the major political parties are tightly controlled. There are too few members of ethnically diverse backgrounds in federal parliament—the same can be said for other factors like gender and age. Despite my critics stating that I am an insider, I very much regard myself as an outsider. I accept that on first glance, my resume appears to be that of an insider—having worked as the acting federal director of the Liberal Party and the Business Council of Australia. I also had multiple shots at preselection. But I am the only sitting federal parliamentarian from New South Wales under forty years of age, the first person in my family to be a member of a political party, growing up in regional Shepparton, and attending public and Catholic schools. I spent a few years trying to get into federal parliament because I wanted to make a policy contribution. My timeline was short. Nearly everyone told me I would need to spend a decade trying to get into the Senate. After a while, I felt that there was a pathway but that was after a number of influential patrons became involved. I am worried that the next person like me will see no pathway because of the complexity, cost, and time involved to win a preselection. That next person could be an Indigenous person lost to the cause. Or, more importantly, lost to the nation's service.

A target for the nation to aim at

Indigenous people constitute 3% of the nation. We should be aiming at least the same proportion in parliament. I say this because we want to ensure we get adequate coverage from each of the parties in Canberra, but also because of the intensive ongoing focus on Indigenous issues. They remain the only group of Australians who have an extensive amount of special laws made on an ongoing basis. There is also the matter of the ongoing connection between the people and the land which calls for a different approach, especially when considering the remoteness of many Aboriginal communities.

As the Senate considered an amendment to the Native Title Act in late 2020, I thought to myself, imagine if we had the Voice up and running. It would be able to provide a summary of advice to the parliament as amendments are proposed. It would be part of the legislation review process—which generally runs through the committees of the Senate, and which has proven to be very effective over fifty years. The bottom line is that having the direct perspective of Indigenous people inside the parliament is crucial. A Voice will only ever be advisory. It will not bind like a parliament can and does. We should have both.

Better than reserved seats

If we fail to hit the target through organic development, there will continue to be debate about the best method for ongoing representation. New Zealand is often put forward as a comparable nation which has long had reserved seats for Maori people. The Parliamentary Library explains that there are

> dedicated seats for Maori, with the number of seats, calculated as a proportion of the Maori population—currently eight seats. Multiple Member Proportional voting (MMP) for a proportion of seats in parliament.

That is, every part of New Zealand has a general electorate

and a Maori electorate. There are separate rolls and Kiwis elect their members of parliament based on their list status. Associate Professor Dominic O'Sullivan says, "In 2017, New Zealand's unicameral parliament has seven designated Maori seats. From 1867 to 2017, Maori have almost always had cabinet membership and a recognised capacity to influence policymaking."

Reserved seats in parliament, along with the Treaty of Waitangi, appear to have contributed to a better fusion of Maori and British culture across the history. This, in turn, is credited by some as leading to better overall social and economic attainment when comparing Indigenous Australians and Maoris. Laura Tingle identifies three factors which have

> changed the cultural and political nature of New Zealand . . . (1) the
> power structures that give Indigenous people a say (2) a recognition
> of wrongs there also came recognition of the value of culture . . . (3)
> there is the power of truth telling of issues resolved for a country.[4]

There is no question that New Zealand has done a better job of capturing the history of Maori. We should do the same and, if we don't, these options from across the ditch will continue to emerge. Jacqui Lambie, a Senator for Tasmania, set out the target of reserving Senate seats for Indigenous people when she was first elected as a Senator for the Palmer United Party. She won't be the last to call for reserved seats.

The Liberal Party

I don't say that we are the only party that needs more Indigenous members. All parties do, but our need is particularly acute. During 2020, Warren Mundine and I were on a panel speaking to the New South Wales Young Liberals about Indigenous policy. We both reflected on the depressing narrative that the Liberals have done very little in the policy space and how that has created very little interest in Liberal politics. In my ten years of active involvement with the New South Wales division, I have met only a handful of Indigenous people, other than Mundine, who have been financial members.

We have had many firsts. The first Indigenous member of federal parliament, the first Indigenous minister, the first Indigenous member of cabinet. Given all these firsts, we should be able to attract Indigenous people to become members of our party.

Active recruitment

In general terms, it is hard to attract new people from all walks of life into political parties. Liberal Party membership was 100,000 in 1945 but is around half that number today. This is a trend away from membership of all organizations.

As Stan Grant and Tim Rowse have observed, there is going to be a middle-class explosion within Indigenous Australia. There are some remarkable statistics. Rowse says between 2006 and 2011, the "proportion of the Indigenous working age population with a post school qualification increased from 39 to 44%." This is a terrific opportunity to bring a new generation of Indigenous people into the Liberal Party—people from all walks of life of course, but with a particular focus on the middle class. After all, the forgotten people of the Menzies era were middle class—the regular salary earners or small businessmen. In modern Australia, the forgotten people are clearly the Indigenous Australians. This was in fact the title of a book put together by Damien Freeman and Shireen

Morris, who published *The Forgotten People* in 2016. Coming before Uluru, their contributors provide diverse centre-right voices making a case for advocacy and action in favour of the Indigenous people of Australia.

I have diagnosed a problem of proximity, where few Australians know or see Indigenous people. This reduces the level of interest Australians have in these matters. It also creates a natural opportunity for Indigenous people to step into leadership roles in my party to reprise the role of Menzies all those decades ago. The party infrastructure was built for this.

I will take it upon myself to attract Indigenous people into the New South Wales division of the Liberal Party. I will also urge the party organization to do all it can to improve membership levels of Indigenous people in each division. This must be more than parachuting Indigenous leaders into winnable positions in the Senate and the House of Representatives. It must be a bottom-up membership drive, so that the perspectives and policy preferences permeate the whole party framework. We need to burnish more interest in the issues facing Indigenous Australians inside the Liberal Party and this is the most obvious method to try. History shows that more members in the rank and file means more members of parliament.

Assessing Uluru

Uluru is an elegant framework. Once the meat is on the bones and it is up and running, how would we assess it? It should be measurable and accountable. How will it complement the Closing the Gap framework and the other suggestions in this book?

It's important that the reforms which emerge from Uluru are properly assessed, especially as a gradual implementation is likely to be forthcoming. On the two elements of the Uluru Statement which I think should be progressed, clear measuring of outcomes and progress could lead to more and better reform. The national Voice could independently evaluate programmes in conjunction with the Productivity Commission. Equally, the truth-telling arrangements could be rolled out further if successful. It all hinges on incorporating a measurement framework of the initial design. Evidence and data are necessary to make a policy case.

Data, data, data

Community level data can be very hard to nail down and it can be vigorously contested for a range of reasons. During December 2020, there was an extensive parliamentary debate about the cashless debit card which was rolled out in Indigenous and non-Indigenous communities alike. Labor, the Greens, and some independent Senators were opposed to the card and explained that one reason was the lack of evidence to support an extension or a widening of the card's application.

The government's Bill did two things: first, it allowed the cashless debit card to remain in the four existing sites in Ceduna, Bundaberg and Hervey Bay, the Goldfields, and East Kimberley until 31 December 2022. The second was to offer a technology upgrade for people who are already on income management in the Northern Territory and Cape York by switching them from the BasicsCard to the cashless debit card.

The Minister for Social Services, Ann Ruston, said at the time,

"The continuation of the Cashless Debit Card program is in direct response to calls from community leaders who tell us that it is ensuring more money is being spent on essentials and supporting positive changes." Ruston admitted that "We definitely have evidence to support that the program is having a positive effect in the community, I just think that we need to get more data." Labor claimed there was no data to support it. Ruston partly agreed—even though there was data from East Kimberly and Ceduna.

The draft study found "clear and consistent evidence alcohol consumption has reduced since the introduction of the CDC, with: 25% of survey respondents (who reported they drink alcohol) reported reducing the amount they drink at any one time, since the Cashless Debit Card's introduction. 22% of survey respondents (who reported they drink alcohol) reported reducing the number of times they drink, since the Cashless Debit Card's introduction."[5] This must not be a feature of the debate following the delivery of the Voice or a national rollout. The data points must be set out and agreed at the outset.

Agreeing to a methodology

What are the key things the Voice is supposed to do? Create community-level engagement, improve policymaking, and provide community-level decision-making. It goes without saying that the key metrics must be the Closing the Gap targets as agreed by the community in partnership with Canberra. The Voice must therefore be measured against how it impacts the Closing the Gap targets. Not all targets will have the same direct community linkage, but the bulk will. For example, target two says: "By 2031, increase the proportion of Aboriginal and Torres Strait Islander babies with a healthy birthweight to 91%."

This target demands the health and maternity services are readily available in the community to match up the objective. Another example, target five is: "By 2031, increase the proportion of Aboriginal and Torres Strait Islander people (age 20-24) attaining year 12 or equivalent qualification to 96%." In the community, this means community control over school buses and ensuring the necessary after school care services are provided to achieve this target. In both the birth weight and year 12 attainment examples, each community should match its starting point on each metric with their own target including a timeframe. Each community is then responsible for its own targets and timetables, and each will be accountable as the Voice is developed. The bottom-up evidence can then be used to demonstrate success (or failure). Ultimately, this can be used as a basis for permanently embedding the Voice in our national life.

This is something that the local and regional Voice organizations can agree and set up themselves but the national Voice must undertake some serious thinking on data collection. Ideally, the national Voice would perform comparisons and analysis of the data to demonstrate good and bad trends. It will also provide swift evidence of performance and underperformance in different regions and localities. We must take heed of the Productivity Commission's advice which challenges the effectiveness of the annual funding for Indigenous Affairs across health, education, and welfare. The Productivity Commission has been critical of accountability, and called for a step-by-step guide for assessing whether money had been well spent.

Community members I meet with agree—many of them tell me they just don't know where the money is going. The Commission's latest review in Indigenous expenditure received 180 submissions and said many programs were developed without adequate consultation with Aboriginal and Torres Strait Islander communities. The Cape York Institute submission said: "Given that the total spend on Indigenous affairs in Australia is nearing $35 billion annually it seems perverse and a measure of the problems, that under the current 'system' monitoring and evaluation does not improve results." Given the lack of support and confidence Canberra has had in Indigenous organizations following the demise of ATSIC, it is most important there are no misgivings about performance evaluation.

An international dataset

The comparison between the Indigenous people of Australia and similar nations—the United States, Canada, and New Zealand should be regularly produced and assessed in Australia. This Australian generated data should complement the collection of the World Council of Indigenous People, which has observer status at the United Nations. Each nation has one key thing in common: an Indigenous community had lived and thrived in each nation prior to European settlement. As set out above, on many of the key statistics, Australia lags far behind the other countries. I first looked into this when some of my parliamentary colleagues chastised me for saying that the Black Lives Matter movement had some important messages for Australia.

Black Lives Matter has reminded us that Indigenous Australians lag behind African Americans in terms of incarceration and lifespan. The national Voice could determine five key data points with each similar nation for comparison, and use these as a basis for regular data collection and reporting.

2067

There are goals we should set for the nation for the centenary of the 1967 referendum.

This book is called *Buraadja*. It means 'tomorrow' in the Dhurga language of the Yuin people of the south coast of New South Wales. I have tried to pull together a policy agenda for tomorrow in this book. I recognise that not everything can be delivered tomorrow, or in the time that I have in federal parliament. I understand that some things will take decades.

But in the context of 60,000 years, what's fifty years? I have set out objectives for the country over the next five decades which culminate in a very important milestone. 2067 will be the centenary of the successful referendum. Once again, it will be an opportunity to reflect on what's been good and bad during the century that Canberra has had the authority to legislate on Indigenous affairs. By 2067, there will have been real progress on the practical and on the symbolic. We need the practical because we have practical issues to solve. And we need symbolic because we will be a stronger and better country by presenting the Australian amalgamation: Indigenous, British, and multicultural. The following sets out my hope for 2067.

Practical

By 2067, the Closing the Gap targets, in place since 2020, will have delivered significant advances in the life of Indigenous people in Australia. Over the decades, the community will have altered the targets to ensure there was genuine accountability for each stakeholder—community, State governments, and federal government. The middle class will have grown and prospered; regenerated, not regressed.

Aboriginal doctors, lawyers, and mathematicians will lead our hospitals, courts, and research facilities. Five percent of the members of the federal parliament are Indigenous. Each major party has at least one Indigenous member. The first Indigenous prime minister was elected at the general election in 2036. In keeping with the firsts of the Liberal Party, the first Indigenous prime minister was indeed a Liberal. In 2030, Australia's Indigenous people surpassed the comparative metrics of the comparable nations. The lower incarceration rate and longer lifespans were linked by data to the local and regional Voice mechanisms set up in the 2020s.

The national Voice has been collecting data on each local region for decades, it has proven to be a successful reform and has been recognised in the nation's Constitution. The Voice has taken on a role of cultural adviser to governments. It has maintained the protocol of the Aboriginal flag but also worked in concert with the Australia Council for the Arts to promote the value of Indigenous culture and art. The Uluru Statement is seen as a turning point as it provided practical options which were implemented over time.

Economic

Indigenous culture and art has become even more prominent within Australia and has become a major export—this has added great value to the nation. The value has been captured by the Indigenous communities. The economic value of Indigenous culture to Australia is unquantifiable. The national Voice has served as an effective cultural adviser to the federal government which has regularly updated intellectual property laws to protect and bolster the industry. There has been no repeat of the appalling treatment of Albert Namatjira and Harold Thomas.

The value of Indigenous ownership of more than half the continent has delivered a large and profitable estate for Indigenous nations which are further away from major centres. In the towns and cities, the consequence of Closing the Gap has meant the day-to-day economic opportunities are equal or better. The review of the land rights laws paved the way for a mix of private and communal custodianship of land and housing which lifted the economic capacity of all Indigenous people by meeting their diverse needs. It also unleashed a new partnership with the private sector where investment in conjunction with traditional owners blossomed into new jobs in the suburbs as well as the remote parts of the continent.

Symbolic

Buraadja Day has been a feature of the national year for decades. Australia Day and Buraadja Day is a staple of the Australian summer, a couple of extra days in the best month of the year to reflect upon our journey as a nation. The National Declaration sits in schools across the nation. In many cases, it sits alongside the

2008 National Apology.

In Canberra, much has changed in the seat of government. The Uluru Statement hangs next to the Barunga Statement in parliament House. Although they hang side-by-side, the Uluru Statement's calls have been addressed, whereas the Barunga Statement's were not. This is important—the Indigenous didn't let the Uluru Statement hang in Parliament House until it was enacted. The cycle of documents ignored by parliament—like the Barunga Statement and the Bark Petitions was finally broken.

The Aboriginal and Torres Strait Island flags are permanently displayed in Parliament House. The Australian flag remains atop Parliament House and in the parliamentary chambers. New statues have been erected in Canberra of Charles Perkins and Neville Bonner. In Perth, there's a city square and a high school named after a man who broke so many firsts, Ken Wyatt. The National Resting Place was established inside the Parliamentary Triangle—on an island in Lake Burley Griffin in between the War Memorial and Old Parliament House. Before the Opening of Parliament each year, the prime minister and opposition leader don a traditional cloak and pay their respects at the resting place. This has been agreed by the traditional owners of the Canberra region—the Ngunnawal people.

Epilogue

No two people are the same and yet some Australians will read this as a book of generalisations. Indigenous Australia is made up of hundreds of nations. Within these diverse groups, there are striking differences depending, for instance, on geography and economic development. The emergence of the Indigenous middle class further complicates the generalisations.

Ultimately, the statistics show that, in the main, Indigenous people lag behind the rest of the nation in terms of incarceration rates, lifespan, educational attainment, and, ultimately, economic development: this is the gap. This is the hole in the Australian project. Closing this gap is a priority. I see it as part of national reconciliation, which encompasses getting to economic parity; providing overdue recognition; and ending the Great Australian Silence in policymaking. The purpose of national reconciliation, as set out in this book, is to deploy institutions and solutions which deliver economically, socially, and symbolically, so that we are a more complete and legitimate nation.

For me, just two words summarise the Indigenous people of Australia: resilience and generosity. There are almost one million Indigenous people in Australia, which is the greatest demonstration of resilience for a people who were expected to die out. The generosity knows no bounds. After nearly 250 years of challenging times, the Indigenous advocates put forward the Uluru Statement, which is a generous contribution to Australia; an opportunity to consolidate Australia. Uluru is a far cry from the extremes of Black Lives Matter. It speaks to unity, not division. Accordingly, this generation must not let the Uluru Statement go the way of the Barunga Statement.

Australian liberalism is big enough and flexible enough to drive this change. And it must. For however long the political class and Indigenous community accept the need for a slew of special laws for Indigenous people, there must be a special system—such as a Voice. To maintain the void is illiberal, which is why the Liberal Party must lead this reform.

Increasingly, Indigenous culture and language is part of our national identity and life. The blooming Indigenous visibility shows we are already living Noel Pearson's tripartite formulation of Australia. Partly, we have Bill Wentworth and the Menzies government to thank. The Australian Institute of Aboriginal and Torres Strait Islander Studies, which they established, has preserved our unique Indigenous history. It has brought to life languages in decline or lost—like the Dhurga language which provided the name for this book.

AIATSIS is a good example of the failure of the liberal movement to mark its historical contribution, which should act as a springboard for future change. That's what this book is about: a liberal case for national reconciliation. By drawing on the enormous contributions of Harold Holt, Malcolm Fraser, and others, the Liberal Party can again deliver historic reform, including a constitutional amendment to recognise ancient Indigenous Australia on our birth certificate. As a parent, I have so much hope for the future of my country and for my children. I hope they will love Australia—I know we need to make it right.

As my inspirational friend, Ken Wyatt, has counselled me, "Patience is a virtue in Aboriginal affairs." It is a privilege to serve with him. He is right—but we have been canvassing meaningful and permanent reconciliation and recognition since John Howard put it on the agenda in 2007. It is long enough. I closed my First Speech to the Senate with these words: "I look forward to writing the next chapter in the rich history of Australian liberalism." This is the chapter I hope we can write together *buraadja*.

Notes

Introduction

1   It is important to acknowledge that both the Victorian legislation of 1855, whose long title was *An Act to Make Provisions for Certain Immigrants*, and the *Immigration Restriction Act 1901* (Cth) were race-based laws—the Victorian law was specifically anti-Chinese.

2   Sir Robert Menzies, *Afternoon Light* (Cassell, 1967), p. 286.

3   See, for example, the expression of Australian liberalism in the twentieth century offered by Menzies in *Afternoon Light*. A useful contemporary summary of Australian liberalism can be found in Tim Wilson's *The New Social Contract: Renewing the liberal vision for Australia* (Kapunda Press, 2020).

4   David Kemp, *The Land of Dreams: How Australians won their freedom 1788-1960* (Miegunyah Press, 2018), p. 485.

5   Noel Pearson, *A Rightful Place*, Quarterly Essay 55, September 2014.

6   Thalia Anthony, "FactCheck Q&A: are Indigenous Australians the most incarcerated people on Earth?", The Conversation, 6 June 2017.

7   Louise Richardson-Self, *Justifying Same-Sex Marriage: A Philosophical Investigation* (Rowman and Littlefield International, 2018).

8   Patrick Dodson, *Beyond the mourning gate: dealing with unfinished business, Wentworth Lecture for 2000* (AIATSIS, 2000).

9   Sir Robert Menzies, Address to Federal Council meeting of the Liberal Party of Australia, Hotel Canberra, 6 April 1964.

10 Kate Slack and Arron Hartnett, "Reflections on the recent High Court decision in *Love v Commonwealth of Australia* [2020] HCA 3", see: <www.higginschambers.com.au/wp-content/uploads/love-and-commonwealth.pdf>.

Bugiya

1   Cassandra Pybus, *Truganini: Journey Through the Apocalypse* (Allen & Unwin, 2020), p. 10.

2   See, for example, Paul Irish, *Hidden in Plain View* (NewSouth, 2017).

3   Commonwealth of Australia, House of Representatives, *Hansard*, 14 August 1963.

4   Commonwealth of Australia, House of Representatives, *Hansard,* 1 May 1962.

5   Paul Daley, "Driving Mr Menzies", *Meanjin,* Vol. 75(1), 2016.

6   Commonwealth of Australia, House of Representatives, *Hansard,* 20 May 1964.

7   Malcolm Mackerras, "How many times do we need to say sorry?" in Damien Freeman and Shireen Morris (eds), *The Forgotten People* (Melbourne University Publishing, 2016), pp. 126-139, p. 130.

8   John Moriarty in conversation with the author, 15 October 2020.

9   Federal Council for the Advancement of Aboriginals, National Petition Campaign Section 51 Clause XXVI (1962): National Museum of Australia Archive.

10   *Ibid.*

11   Billy Snedden, Submission to Cabinet, 22 February 1965.

12   Harold Holt, "Referendum—Statement by the Prime Minister", media release, 15 February 1967.

13   Tony Eggleton in conversation with the author, 28 October 2020.

14   Nigel Bowen, Submission to Cabinet, 22 February 1967.

15   *Ibid.*

16   Harold Holt, News Conference, Mascot Airport, 28 May 1967.

17   Ian Sinclair in conversation with the author, 22 December 2020.

18   Tony Eggleton in conversation with the author, 28 October 2020.

19   Ian Sinclair in conversation with the author, 22 December 2020.

20   Robert Holt in conversation with the author, 28 November 2020.

21   Troy Bramston, *The Australian,* 4 November 2013.

22   *Ibid.*

23   Letter from the Federal Council for the Advancement of Aboriginals to Harold Holt, 1967.

24   Tony Eggleton in conversation with the author, 27 October 2020.

25   Angela Burger, *Neville Bonner: A Biography* (MacMillan, 1979), p. 51.

26   *Ibid.*

27   *Ibid.,* p. 59.

28   *Ibid.,* p. 78.

29   Ian Viner in conversation with the author, 17 December 2020.

30   Tom Frame, *The Life and Death of Harold Holt* (Allen & Unwin, 2005), p. 214.

31   See: Sarah Pritchard, "The 'Race' Power in Section 51(xxvi) of the Constitution", *Australian Indigenous Law Review,* Vol. 15(2), 2011, p. 49: "Significant post-1967 legislation enacted by the Commonwealth Parliament in reliance on section 51(xxvi) has included the Aboriginal Land Rights (Northern Territory) Act 1976, the World Heritage Properties Conservation Act 1983, the Aboriginal and Torres Strait Islander Heritage Protection Act 1984, the Native Title Act 1993, and the

Corporations (Aboriginal and Torres Strait Islander) Act 2006."

32 Tom Frame, *Harold Holt and the Liberal Imagination* (Connor Court, 2018), p. 83.

33 Tony Eggleton in conversation with the author, 27 October 2020.

34 *The Life and Death of Harold Holt*, p. 166.

35 Chris Puplick in conversation with the author, 23 December 2020.

36 Margaret Simons and Malcolm Fraser, *Malcolm Fraser: The Political Memoirs* (Miegunyah Press, 2010), p. 385.

37 *Ibid.*, p. 401.

38 Fred Chaney in conversation with the author, 26 November 2020.

39 Ian Sinclair in conversation with the author, 22 December 2020.

40 Chris Puplick in conversation with the author, 23 December 2020.

41 *Malcolm Fraser: The Political Memoirs,* p. 398.

42 Peter Baume in conversation with the author, 23 November 2020.

43 *Malcolm Fraser: The Political Memoirs*, p. 391.

44 Phillip Ruddock in conversation with the author, 13 October 2020.

45 Ian Viner, Address to National Press Club, 7 July 1977.

46 Ian Viner in conversation with the author, 17 December 2020.

47 *Ibid.*

48 Peter Baume in conversation with the author, 23 November 2020.

49 Fred Chaney in conversation with the author, 26 November 2020.

50 Ian Viner, Address to National Press Club, 7 July 1977.

51 Ian Viner in conversation with the author, 17 December 2020.

52 *Malcolm Fraser: The Political Memoirs,* p. 392.

53 Ian Viner in conversation with the author, 17 December 2020.

54 *Malcolm Fraser: The Political Memoirs,* p. 399.

55 Peter Baume in conversation with the author, 23 November 2020.

56 *Ibid.*

57 See J. Fenley, "The National Aboriginal Conference and the Makarrata: Sovereignty and Treaty Discussions, 1979–81", *Australian Historical Studies*, Vol. 42, 2011, pp. 375–378; R. Nichols (Chairman, NAC), "A summary of concerns of the Aboriginal People of Australia", presentation to World Assembly of First Nations, Regina, Canada, 1982, reprinted in B. Attwood and A. Markus, *The Struggle for Aboriginal Rights* (Allen & Unwin, 1999), pp. 297–301.

58 Commonwealth of Australia, *Two Hundred Years Later... Report by the Senate Standing Committee on Constitutional and Legal Affairs on the feasibility of a compact, or 'Makarrata', between the Commonwealth and Aboriginal people*, 1983, pp. 17-18.

59 Malcolm Fraser, Vincent Lingiari Lecture, Charles Darwin University, 24 August 2000.

60 Paul Kelly, *The March of Patriots: The Struggle for Modern Australia* (Melbourne University Press, 2009), p. 341.

61 Pamela Williams, *The Victory: The Inside Story of the Takeover of Australia* (Allen & Unwin, 1997), p. 46.

62 *The March of Patriots*, p. 343.

63 *Ibid.*, p. 357.

64 Geoffrey Blainey, "Drawing up a balance sheet of our history", *Quadrant,* July-August 1993, pp. 10-15.

65 Ann Curthoys, *Freedom Rides* (Oxford University Press, 2006).

66 *The March of Patriots*, p. 346.

67 John Howard, Address to the Sydney Institute, 11 October 2007.

68 Letter from Noel Pearson to John Howard, as cited by Kelly in *The March of Patriots.*

69 Tony Abbott, *Battlelines* (Melbourne University Press, 2013), p. 166.

70 Damien Freeman, "Understanding where they're coming from" in Damien Freeman and Shireen Morris, *The Forgotten People* (Melbourne University Publishing, 2016), pp. 172-178, p. 175.

71 Tony Abbott, Address at the Garma Festival, August 2013.

72 Malcolm Turnbull, *A Bigger Picture* (Hardie Grant Books, 2020), p. 561.

73 *Ibid.,* p. 563.

74 Malcolm Turnbull interview with Karla Grant, Living Black: NITV, 16 June 2020.

75 *A Bigger Picture,* p. 571.

76 Malcolm Turnbull in conversation with author, 18 December 2020.

77 W. E. H. Stanner, *After the Dreaming: The Boyer Lectures* (ABC, 1968), p. 26.

78 Anna Clark, The Conversation, 3 August 2018.

79 Damien Freeman, "The glory of your great yesterday" in *Hope in Common: regaining confidence in democracy* (forthcoming).

2 Nhaway

1 Pluckrose and Lindsay, *Cynical Theories* (Pitchstone Publishing, 2020).

2 Warren Mundune, "It's the Economy, Stupid: Economic Participation Only Way to Close the Gap", *Analysis Papers,* 14 July 2020 (Centre for Independent Studies).

3 Minerals Council of Australia, Submission to the Joint Standing Committee on Northern Australia into Juukan Gorge, 19 August 2020.

4   Commonwealth of Australia, *Never Again: Joint Parliamentary Committee into Juukan Gorge Interim Report,* December 2020.

5   "Hierarchy of Needs", *The Economist,* 13 October 2008.

6   Jacinta Price, *The Australian,* 9 March 2020.

7   United States data from Center for Disease Control and Prevention supplied by Parliamentary Library.

8   Brooke Boney in conversation with the author, 14 January 2021.

9   Marcia Langton in conversation with the author, 17 December 2020.

10 National Indigenous Australians Agency, submission to the Senate Select Committee on the Aboriginal Flag, established 3 September 2020.

11 Marcia Langton, transcript of evidence to the Senate Select Committee on the Aboriginal Flag, 24 September 2020.

12 Sir Robert Menzies, *Afternoon Light* (Cassell, 1967).

13 David Furse-Roberts (ed.), *Howard: The Art of Persuasion* (Connor Court, 2018), p. 250.

14 Laura Tingle, *The High Road: What Australia Can Learn from New Zealand,* Quarterly Essay 80, 2020, p. 31.

15 Terri Janke, *Guarding Ground: A Vision for a National Indigenous Cultural Authority, Wentworth Lecture* (AIATSIS, 2008).

16 Response from Department of Parliamentary Services supplied by the Parliamentary Library.

17 Pluckrose and Lindsay, p. 253.

18 Pat Turner, Address to the National Press Club of Australia, 30 September 2020.

19 Stan Grant in conversation with the author, 21 December 2020.

20 Michael Mansell, National Indigenous Television, 15 July 2019.

21 Ian Viner, Address to National Press Club, 7 July 1977.

22 Don Watson, *Recollections of a Bleeding Heart: A Portrait of Paul Keating* (Random House, 2002), p. 547.

23 Phillip Ruddock, Statement on Good Governance and Conflict of Interest in ATSIC, 17 April 2003.

24 Peter Costello and Peter Coleman, *The Costello Memoirs* (Melbourne University Press, 2009), p. 214.

25 Margaret Simons and Malcolm Fraser, *Malcolm Fraser: The Political Memoirs* (Miegunyah Press, 2010), p. 411.

26 Marcia Langton in conversation with the author, 17 December 2020.

27 Malcolm Turnbull, *A Bigger Picture* (Hardie Grant Books, 2020), p. 571.

28 Malcolm Turnbull, media statement, 26 October 2017.

29 Malcolm Turnbull interview with Karla Grant, *Living Black: NITV,* 16 June 2020.

30 Malcolm Turnbull in conversation with the author, 18 December 2020.

31 *The Australian*, 28 June 2017.

32 *The Guardian,* 18 July 2019.

33 Commonwealth of Australia, Final Report of the Joint Select Committee on Constitutional Recognition relating to Aboriginal and Torres Strait Islander Peoples, November 2018, p. xvii.

34 *Ibid.*, p. xviii.

35 Liberal Party of Australia, *Our plan to support Indigenous Australians,* Liberal Party policy document for 2019 election, issued 15 May 2019.

36 Nigel Scullion, *The Guardian,* 5 April 2019.

37 Danny Gilbert, "The Torment of Powerlessness", Address to the Garma Festival, 7 August 2019.

38 Noel Pearson, Foreword to Damien Freeman and Shireen Morris (eds), *The Forgotten People* (Melbourne University Publishing, 2016), p. xiv.

39 Graham Bradley, "Towards a winning referendum proposal" in Damien Freeman and Shireen Morris (eds), *The Forgotten People* (Melbourne University Publishing, 2016), pp. 115-125, p. 122.

40 Anne Twomey, The Conversation, 20 May 2015.

41 Professor Anne Twomey in conversation with the author, 6 February 2021.

42 Submission by Pat Anderson, Megan Davis, Noel Pearson et al. to the Joint Select Committee on Constitutional Recognition Relating to Aboriginal and Torres Strait Islander Peoples.

43 Anne Twomey, The Conversation, 8 July 2020.

44 Professor Anne Twomey in conversation with the author, 6 February 2021.

45 A Voice would not be in Chapter III of the Constitution because it would not be part of the Judiciary.

46 Marcia Langton in conversation with the author, 17 December 2020.

47 Tim Rowse, *Indigenous and Other Australians Since 1901* (UNSW Press, 2017), p. 287.

48 Harry Hobbs and George Williams, "The Noongar Settlement: Australia's First Treaty", *Sydney Law Review,* Vol. 40(1), 2018, p. 1ff.

49 Letter from Doug Nicholls to Ben Chifley in 1949 supplied by the Parliamentary Library.

50 Commonwealth of Australia, House of Representatives, *Hansard,* 14 August 1963.

51 National Aboriginal Conference, 1979.

52 Galarrwuy Yunupingu, "Rom Watangu", *The Monthly,* 1 July 2016.

53 Hobbs and Williams, *supra.*

54 "Noongar 2020", see: <www.noongar.org.au>.

55 Ken Colbung, *Not Land Rights, But Land Rites, Wentworth Lecture* (AIATSIS, 1988).

56 Stan Grant, *The Australian,* 15 May 2020.

57 Marcia Langton in conversation with the author, 17 December 2020.

58 Brooke Boney in conversation with the author, 14 January 2021.

59 David Kemp, *The Land of Dreams* (Miegunyah Press, 2018), p. 172.

60 *Ibid.*

61 Stan Grant, *Australia Day* (Harper Collins 2019), p. 33.

62 *Malcolm Fraser: The Political Memoirs,* p. 568.

63 James Haughton and Apolline Kohen, *Aboriginal and Torres Strait Islander treaties, constitutional and legal recognition and representation in Australia: a chronology,* Parliamentary Library Research Paper Series, 2019-20, pp. 12.

64 E-mail message from Ivan Roberts to the author, 8 January 2021.

3 Burradja

1 Anne Twomey, "The Preamble and Indigenous Recognition", *Australian Indigenous Law Review,* Vol. 15(2), 2011, pp. 4-22.

2 Sir Harry Gibbs, *A Preamble: The Issues* (Samuel Griffith Society, 1999).

3 Commonwealth of Australia, *Recognising Aboriginal and Torres Strait Islander Peoples in the Constitution: Report of the Expert Panel,* 2012, p. 119.

4 Laura Tingle, *The High Road: What Australia Can Learn from New Zealand,* Quarterly Essay 80, 2020, p. 37-38.

5 Department of Social Services, Future of Employment and Skills Research Centre, University of Adelaide, 2020.

Index

THE KAPUNDA PRESS

GENERAL EDITOR
Damien Freeman
PM Glynn Institute
Australian Catholic University

Forthcoming

SHADOW OF THE CROSS
CATHOLIC SOCIAL TEACHING AND AUSTRALIAN POLITICS
Greg Craven
Kevin Rudd – Tony Abbott – Maurice Glasman – Sandra Cornish
Philip Booth

2020

FAITH'S PLACE
DEMOCRACY IN A RELIGIOUS WORLD
Bryan S. Turner – Damien Freeman
Dean Smith – Luke Gosling – Ursula Stephens – Jocelyne Cesari
Jim Franklin – Robert Hefner – Riaz Hassan – David Saperstein
M. A. Casey

THE NEW SOCIAL CONTRACT
RENEWING THE LIBERAL VISION FOR AUSTRALIA
Tim Wilson

TRIBALISM'S TROUBLES
RESPONDING TO ROWAN WILLIAMS
Damien Freeman
Rowan Williams – Ethan Westwood – M. A. Casey – Cristina Gomez
Nigel Zimmermann – Annette Pierdziwol – Kerry Pinkstone
Amanda Stoker – Scott Stephens – Ben Etherington
Anthony Ekpo – Austin Wyatt – Sandra Jones

2019
STORY OF OUR COUNTRY
LABOR'S VISION FOR AUSTRALIA
Adrian Pabst

THE MARKET'S MORALS
RESPONDING TO JESSE NORMAN
Damien Freeman
Jesse Norman – Marc Stears – Greg Melleuish – Adrian Pabst
Amanda Walsh – Parnell McGuinness – Michael Easson
David Corbett – Tom Switzer – Cris Abbu – Tanya Aspland
Leanne Smith – M. A. Casey

NONSENSE ON STILTS
RESCUING HUMAN RIGHTS IN AUSTRALIA
Damien Freeman – Catherine Renshaw
M. A. Casey – Nicholas Aroney – Emma Dawson
Terri Butler – Jennifer Cook – Bryan Turner – Tim Wilson

FEDERATION'S MAN OF LETTERS
PATRICK MCMAHON GLYNN
Anne Henderson
Anne Twomey – Suzanne Rutland
Patrick Mullins – John Fahey – Peter Boyce

2018
TODAY'S TYRANTS
RESPONDING TO DYSON HEYDON
Damien Freeman
J. D. Heydon – Frank Brennan – Anne Henderson – Paul Kelly
M. A. Casey – Peter Kurti – M. J. Crennan – Hayden Ramsay
Shireen Morris – Michael Ondaatje – Sandra Lynch – Catherine Renshaw

CHALICE OF LIBERTY
PROTECTING RELIGIOUS FREEDOM IN AUSTRALIA
Frank Brennan – M. A. Casey – Greg Craven

9 781922 449542